# French Letters to Write

Enjoy your property buying and renovation experience by using the letters from this book to cope with the horrendous bureaucracy of the French system. The nightmare of coping with the rigid formality of France becomes much easier with this simple resource.

You may not find the perfect letter immediately but you can always copy sections from different pages to combine them together to say exactly what you mean. Most letters have singular and plural options together with various action options and where appropriate different styles of address are shown for professionals.

With this book you can confidently find the words you need for dealing with house buying and ownership, responding to situations with notaires and the Mairie. Organise your home, motoring and renovation needs. They are all covered in the following pages.

**British Library Cataloguing in Publication Data**
A catalogue record of this book is available from the British Library.


ISBN  1-84685-410-5
978-1-84685-410-0

Published 2006 by

Redbarn Publishing *in association with*
Exposure Publishing, an imprint of Diggory Press,
Three Rivers, Minions, Liskeard, Cornwall, PL14 5LE, UK




Redbarn Publishing, Redbarn, Swindon SN4 9LT, England.
www.frenchletters.com

Written and compiled from an idea by Gordon Hayward who recognised the need for a book of letters shortly after buying a small cottage in France.

Translated by Jean Quiercelan, who retired after many years in business as a land and property surveyor. Jean's patience and attention to detail has brought an unusual accuracy to the finished French letters which retain the original English meaning but with a distinct French flavour.

Edited by Valou Calder a native French translator who abandoned life on a champage vineyard to marry an Englishman. Needless to say they have their own French home and spend as much time there as their busy lives allow.

London – Paris outline drawn by Gemma Jeffery

# French Letters to Write

This collection of letters has been written to try to make buying and owning a French property a more pleasant experience. Nothing is more frustrating than having a situation that, in your own country would require nothing more than a simple phone call or letter. We can't help with the phone call but these letters provide an excellent starter for many varied situations.

Few people can write a fluent letter in a foreign language and this edition is a starter to get you going. Many of the paragraphs from different letters can be interchanged to enable you to create your personalised letter.

Written by a frustrated buyer who recognised his own language shortcomings and translated by Jean Quiercelan who wrote many letters on his behalf to get things moving.

You will notice that the simple 'Yours faithfully' or 'Yours sincerely' translates to a much longer and more flowery prose in French which is, of course, correct French grammar. You will also notice that a sentence appears thanking the recipient for his time and effort, this is normal business practice in France. Again there are words that when translated in to French lose the appearance of being polite and if used in English would be regarded as downright rude. Try the simple phrase 'I ask' and you get 'Je demande' – you really are asking and not demanding!   Many of the translations are not word for word but have been chosen to ensure that the meaning always remains the same.

There will be many subjects that you will want covered that are not here, now you have the opportunity to contribute to next years edition by drafting a sample letter, in English, you would like to see included and emailing it to the author at  new@frenchletters.com .

Enjoy your house in France.

## Inserting accents using Word

French accents can be a problem when you are writing a letter using an English keyboard. Fortunately, when you use Word as your word processor the problem is easily solved. Just use the out code facility that is built in to the programme.

Sounds complicated but just look up the letter with the appropriate accent and remember the number. Place the cursor where you want the letter, press and hold down the Alt key and on the number pad type in the number. As soon as you release the Alt key the character will appear.

| | | | | | | | | |
|---|---|---|---|---|---|---|---|---|
| à | = | altkey | + | 0133 | Ê | = | alt key | + | 0210 |
| À | = | alt key | + | 0183 | ë | = | alt key | + | 0137 |
| â | = | alt key | + | 0160 | Ë | = | alt key | + | 0211 |
| Â | = | alt key | + | 0181 | ï | = | alt key | + | 0139 |
| â | = | alt key | + | 0131 | î | = | alt key | + | 0140 |
| â | = | alt key | + | 0132 | ô | = | alt key | + | 0147 |
| À | = | alt key | + | 0142 | ô | = | alt key | + | 0148 |
| à | = | alt key | + | 0198 | Ô | = | alt key | + | 0153 |
| Â | = | alt key | + | 0199 | ù | = | alt key | + | 0151 |
| è | = | alt key | + | 0138 | ii | = | alt key | + | 0129 |
| È | = | alt key | + | 0212 | U | = | alt key | + | 0154 |
| é | = | alt key | + | 0130 | û | = | alt key | + | 0150 |
| É | = | alt key | + | 0144 | ç | = | alt key | + | 0135 |
| ê | = | alt key | + | 0136 | Ç | = | alt key | + | 0128 |

Too fiddly? You can always change the keyboard by purchasing a French keyboard when you are in France and enjoy using an ASWERTY keypad when you are used to a QWERTY layout!

With your computer switched off, unplug the English keyboard and replace it with the French version.

Go to the computer "Control Panel", select "Keyboard" and add French to the keyboards available. You can also select the keys to toggle between French and English. Depending on your computer you may be asked to insert the windows cd

Can't find the € sign – Hold down **Ctrl** and **Alt** at the same time and then press **4**

The best solution is to download the Languages Toolbar from our web site

**www.frenchletters.com**

## Installing and using the accent's toolbar for Word

When you have unzipped (or extracted) the file accents.zip you will see this image. Double click on the Setup Icon

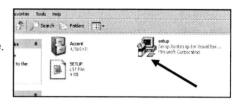

Click the Run button

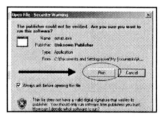

Click the OK button

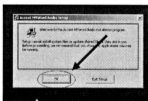

Click the Install button

And a few seconds later you have a toolbar to insert all of the accents you need to write a perfect letter in French - Acute, Grave, Cedilla, Circumflex.... 31 in all.

Just type your letter and when you want an accented character just touch the accent you want and it is instantly inserted where the cursor is placed.

**Download it now from www.frenchletters.com**

# Letter Subjects

## Banking and Money

## Artisans

## Materials, Plant & Tool Hire

## The Mairie

## Employment

## Cars and Driving

## Medical

## Schools

## Insurance

## Accommodation

## Pets

## Social

# Opening and Closing letters

Your opening phrase in a letter written in French sets the tone of the letter and has a great bearing on the closing line. A few of the common opening phrases are show here, together with appropriate closing phrases. They are not literal translations but the nearest that the French use as equivalents. You will no doubt notice the phrase in English tends to be much shorter!

## Business Letters

| | |
|---|---|
| Dear Sir,<br>Yours faithfully, | Monsieur,<br>Je vous prie d'agréer, Monsieur, l'assurance de ma considération distinguee. |
| Dear Sirs,<br>Yours faithfully, | Messieurs,<br>Je vous prie d'agréer, Monsieurs, l'assurance de ma considération distinguée. |
| To whom it may concern<br>Yours faithfully, | Monsieur \ Madame,<br>Je vous prie d'agréer, Monsieur, l'assurance de ma considération distinguée. |
| Dear Mr. Jones,<br>Yours sincerely, | Cher Monsieur Jones,<br>Je vous prie de croire, Monsieur Jones, à mes sincères salutations. |
| Dear Mrs. Jones,<br>Yours sincerely, | Chère Madame Jones,<br>Je vous prie de croire, Madam Jones, à mes sincères salutations. |
| Dear Miss Jones,<br>Yours sincerely, | Chère Mademoiselle Jones<br>Je vous prie de croire, Mademoiselle Jones, à mes sincères salutations. |

There are many different closing phrases used in French and the few shown are the more commonly used in general business letters. You will be able to reply to letters you receive by using the same or similar closing words to the one sent to you. Be careful to change (ma \ mon \ mes) to agree with the gender of the writer.

## Semi-formal Letters

When you do not know the person, this style is appropriate. The choice is yours as to whether you use the person's surname where you are aware of it.

Open your letter with one of the following

| | |
|---|---|
| Dear Sir | Monsieur, |
| Dear Madam | Madame |
| Dear Miss | Mademoiselle |
| Dear Mr. Pierce | Monsieur Pierce |
| Dear Mrs. Pierce | Madame Pierce |
| Dear Miss Pierce | Mademoiselle Pierce |

Close your letter with one of the following:

| | |
|---|---|
| Best wishes | Je vous envoie mes bien amicales pensées. |
| Yours sincerely | Recevez, je vous prie, mes meilleures amitiés. |
| Kind regards | Je vous adresse mon très amical souvenir. |

## Personal letters

| | |
|---|---|
| Dear George | Cher George, |
| Dear Annette | Chère Annette, |
| Dear George and Annette | Chers George et Annette, |
| Dear Grandparents | Chers grands-parents, |
| My Dearest George | Mon cher George |
| My Dearest Annette | Ma chère Annette |
| Dear friend  (male) | Cher ami, |
| Dear friend  (female) | Chère amie |
| Dear Friends | Chers amis |
| | |
| Sincerely yours | Cordialement à vous |
| Your friend | Amitiés |
| In friendship | Bien amicalement |
| With kind regards | Chaleureusement |
| Best wishes | Bien à toi |
| Best wishes to all | Bien des choses à tous |
| See you soon | A bientôt |
| Lots of love | Bons baisers |

## Get Property details

French agents can be found by using an internet search, www.pagesjaunes.fr. local newspapers or using your shoe leather.

25 The Groves
25 The Groves
Winchester
Hampshire
WR7 9PP

22nd March, 2006

Century 21
Agent Immobilier
4 rue du Parc
64566 - Montpellier

Dear Sirs,

(I \ We \ My wife and I \ My partner and I) are looking for a house (to renovate \ that need small improvements \ is in good condition, ready to move in \ that is livable) in the Montpellier South area and a radius of 20 km.

The property should be in a (small town \ large city \ rural village \ isolated). Ground floor accommodation should have a minimum of 3 living rooms, 1 kitchen, bathroom and toilet). A minimum of 3 bedrooms are required. The land are should be 2000 sq metres and adjoining the property. The property should be on (mains sewerage \connected to a septic tank system). Telephone, water, gas and electricity should be connected or available.

Please advise me of any properties you have that appear to fit this specification and send details to me (us) by (post \ email at g.broughton @frenchletters.com \ fax at +44 1793 222222).

(I \ We) propose to visit  20\04\2006 to 30\04\2006 and (I \ we) will contact you when we have selected suitable properties to view.


Yours faithfully,



Gérard and Marion Broughton

All of the options are in the same order as the English version. Make sure you change all of the number options for rooms.

Gérard and Marion Broughton
25 The Groves
Winchester
Hampshire
WR7 9PP

Winchester, le 22 mars 2006

Century 21
Agent Immobilier
4 rue du Parc
64566 - Montpellier

Monsieur,

(Je recherche \ Ma femme et moi recherchons \ Ma partenaire et moi recherchons) une maison (à rénover \ demandant peu de travaux \ en bon état - prête à emménager \ habitable) dans la région de Montpellier Sud et dans un rayon de 20 kilomètres.

Cette propriété est à prévoir dans (une petite ville \ une grande ville \ un village rural \ isolé). Le rez-de-chaussée doit comprendre 3 salles de séjour, 1 cuisine, 1 salle de bain et des toilettes. Cette maison devra avoir au minimum 3 chambres. Prévoir un terrain autour d'environ 2000 mètres carrés. Cette propriété devra avoir (le tout à l'égout \ être connectée à une fosse septique) - Connections actuelles ou possibilité formelle de connections aux réseaux téléphonique, eau potable, gaz et électricité.

Voudriez-vous avoir l'amabilité de (me \ nous) soumettre un choix des propriétés ayant les caractéristiques demandées ci-dessus par (poste \ e-mail: g.broughton @frenchletters.com \ fax : +44 1793 222222).

(Je me propose \ Nous nous proposons) de nous rendre dans la région du 20\04\2006 au 30\04\2006 et de prendre contact avec vous dès que vous (m' \ nous) aurez adressé le résultat de vos recherches pour les visiter.

En cette attente et avec (mes \ nos) remerciements anticipés, veuillez agréer, Monsieur, l'expression de (mes \ nos) sentiments les meilleurs.

Gérard et Marion Broughton.

## Make an Offer for a Property

Select the numbered paragraphs you require and delete the rest. Be very careful to insert your property name, location and price and take care with (singular \ plural) choices

25 The Groves
Winchester
Hampshire
WR7 9PP

Monsieur G. PREMONT                                    22nd November, 2006
Euro Immobilier
4 rue du Parc
75000 - PARIS

Dear Mr. Premont

1.  Thank you for your time in accompanying us to visit properties (recently \ date.)

2.  (I \ We) wish to make an offer of 122,000 euros for the property "Le Petit Bois, Vautorte". Would you please arrange for the initial contract to be sent to (me \ us) as soon as the vendor has accepted the offer.

3.  The following conditions are required to be inserted in the contract:

4.  The offer is subject to obtaining a satisfactory mortgage offer by 15 December 2006.

5.  Confirmation of availability of (gas \ electricity \ water \ telephone) connections and the price to connect.

6.  Confirmation that planning consents claimed are approved by the council and are valid for 12 months or are renewable. ◄——— Insert period of months

7.  (I \ We) would like completion to be on or about   15th January, 2006 (and would like the vendor notaire to act for (me \ us.)

8.  (I \ We) would like completion to be on or about   15th January, 2006 and will be using my own notaire  Maître Foulrard, at Laval who will contact you with any additional suspension clauses that are required.)

Yours faithfully,

John and Janice Clewis

John et Marion Clewis
25 The Groves
Winchester
Hampshire
WR7 9PP
Winchester, le 22 novembre 2006

Monsieur G. PREMONT
Euro Immobilier
4 rue du Parc
75000 - PARIS

Cher Monsieur PREMONT

(Je vous remercie \ Nous vous remercions) de (m'avoir guidé \ nous avoir guidés) dans la visite des propriétés à vendre - (récemment \ le 10 novembre).

(Je voudrais \ Nous voudrions ) faire une offre de 122000 euros pour la propriété sise au lieudit " le Petit Bois " commune de Vautorte. Voudriez-vous avoir l'amabilité d'étudier un compromis de vente et de (me \ nous) le faire parvenir dès que le vendeur aura accepté cette offre.

(Je joins \ Nous joignons) à ce pli la liste des conditions que (j'aimerais \ nous aimerions) inclure dans le compromis.

Cette offre est faite sous la condition suspensive d'obtention du prêt nécessaire à cette acquisition sollicité le 15 décembre 2006.

Confirmation de la possibilité de branchement aux réseaux de (gaz \ électricité \ eau \ téléphone) et du coût de ces branchements ou connections.

Confirmation que ce projet est approuvé sans réserve par l'administration et reste valable durant (xx mois) (années) ou par tacite reconduction.

(J'aimerais \ Nous aimerions) que la signature de l'acte notarié intervienne aux environs du 15 janvier 2006 sous l'office unique du notaire du vendeur.

(J'aimerais \ Nous aimerions) que la signature de l'acte notarié intervienne aux environs du 15 janvier 2006 et (je demande \ nous demandons ) l'intervention de (mon \ notre ) Notaire  Maître Fourlard  demeurant à Laval que vous pourrez contacter pour les différentes conditions non prévues dans cette lettre.

Recevez (mes \ nos) remerciements anticipés pour la bonne suite que vous voudrez bien donner à ce projet,

(Je vous prie d'agréer \ Nous vous prions) d'agréer, cher (Monsieur \ Maître), l'expression de nos meilleurs sentiments.

Estate Agent              Notaire

John Clewis                 Janice Clewis

## Make a viewing Appointment

French agents are a lot skimpier on property details and will expect you to sign a "bon de visite" before you view any properties.

25 The Groves
Winchester
Hampshire
WR7 9PP

22nd March, 2006

Century 21
Agent Immobilier
4 rue du Parc
64566 – Montpellier

(Dear Sir \Mrs Maritas \ Mr. Maritas),

Thank you for sending the selection of properties as requested. (I \ We) (have seen properties on your web site \ in your window display) ref: MYN2346 , MYN2349 and we would like you to arrange viewing appointments for (myself \ us).

We will be available to view properties (all day \ morning \ afternoon) on the following dates 4th October 2006, 5th October 2006 and 7th October 2006.

During our time in France (I \ we) will be available by (telephone +44 1793 222222 \ email : Gerard @frenchletters.com \ post : Le perron, St Jean, 53500 Laval).

Yours faithfully,

Gérard and Marion Broughton

All of the options are in the same order as the English version. Make sure you change all options and that reference numbers are exact.

Gérard et Marion Broughton
25 The Groves
Winchester
Hampshire
WR7 9PP

Winchester, le 22 mars 2006

Century 21
Agent Immobilier
4 rue du Parc
64566 -
Montpellier

Cher Monsieur, Chère Madame Maritas \ Cher Monsieur Maritas,

(Je vous remercie \ Nous vous remercions) infiniment de nous avoir envoyé une sélection de propriétés correspondant à ce que nous recherchons.

(J'ai \ Nous avons) vu des propriétés sur (votre site internet \ dans votre vitrine ) réf: MYN2346 , réf: MYN2349 et (je voudrais \ nous voudrions ) prendre rendez-vous pour les visiter.

Nous pouvons visiter ces propriétés (dans la journée \ le matin \ l'après-midi) aux dates suivantes: les 4, 5 ou 7 octobre 2006.

Pendant notre séjour en France vous pouvez (me \ nous) joindre par (téléphone au  +44 1793 222222 \ par adresse e-mail: Gerard @ frenchletters.com \ par courrier: Le perron, St Jean, 53500 Laval).

Avec (mes \ nos) remerciements anticipés, veuillez agréer, (chère Madame \ cher Monsieur Maritas), l'expression de (mes \ nos ) sentiments les meilleurs.


Gérard et Marion Broughton

# Seven Day Cooling Off Period

When you sign the initial Compromis de Vente you have a seven day cooling off period during which you can change your mind and receive your deposit back in full.

The letter must be received by the vendor \ vendor's notaire \ estate agent within seven days of signing the Compromis de Vente.

Text in brackets is shown with the style set as (Singular \ Plural)
If letter is to a Notaire insert the wording from the grey framed boxes to replace the style used for an Estate Agent (Immobilier).

25 The Groves
Winchester
Hampshire
WR7 9PP

22nd March, 2006

Monsieur G. PREMONT
Agent Immobilier
4 rue du Parc
75000 - PARIS

Dear Sirs

### Le Petit Bois, 65789 Montpellier - Cancellation of contract

(I \ We)  give formal notice that  under La Loi SRU  which gives a seven day cooling off period (I \ we) rescind the Compromis de Vente signed on 19\03\2006  relating to the above property.

Please return the deposit paid immediately.

Yours faithfully,

John Clewis                    Janice Clewis

Text in brackets is shown with the style set as (Singular \ Plural). Delete the singular or plural as required and remove brackets.

Text in boxes should be used when writing to a notaire.

Maître  Laurence
Notaire
Place de Paris
76500 Montpellier

John  et Janice Clewis
25 The Groves
Winchester
Hampshire
WR7 9PP

Winchester, le 22 mars 2006

Monsieur G. PREMONT
Agent Immobilier
4 rue du Parc
75000 - PARIS

Objet : Projet d'acquisition de (address of property in contract )
suivant compromis de vente signé le 19\03\2006. à votre Agence

à votre Etude

Cher Monsieur,          Cher Maître

(J'ai \ Nous avons) le regret de vous informer que, conformément à la Loi SRU, (je renonce \ nous renonçons) à l'acquisition de la propriété citée en référence.

En conséquence, (je vous serais oblige \ nous vous serions obligés) de (me \ nous) restituer immédiatement le dépôt de garantie que (je vous ai \ nous vous avons) réglé.

Avec (mes \ nos) remerciements anticipés pour votre compréhension et votre diligence, veuillez agréer, cher (Monsieur \ Maître) l'expression de (mes \ nos) sentiments distingués.

John Clewis                                      Janice Clewis

## Estate Agents Fees

Make sure you know what, if any, fees are included in the price quoted for the property. Agents vary as to how they offer properties and with agents fees in the 6% to 10% range and notaires fees of up to 11% you really need to be sure.

Le Petit Bois
53567 Laval

2nd May, 2006

Mr. G. PREMONT
Agent Immobilier
4 rue du Parc
75000 - PARIS

Dear Mr. PREMONT,

Thank you for details of property ref: L1234\S56

Could you please explain if the quoted price is all fees inclusive, agents and notaires fees, agents fees only or no fees included.

(I \ We) would appreciate a detailed breakdown of any fees that would be expected with the purchase of this property.

Yours faithfully,

John and Mary Matthews

Remember to insert the property reference in place of the reference shown and remove the singular or plural where shown (singular \ plural).

John et Mary Matthews
Le Petit Bois
53567 Laval

Laval, le 2 mai 2006

Monsieur G. PREMONT
Agent Immobilier
4 rue du Parc
75000 - PARIS

Cher Monsieur Premont,

Merci pour les renseignements que vous (m'avez \ nous avez) adressés concernant la propriété ref: L1234\S56

Voudriez vous (me \ nous) dire si le prix noté inclus tous les frais, négociation d'agence et frais d'acte, ou seulement la commission d'agence ou s'il s'agit du prix vendeur, tous les frais en plus ?

(J'aimerais \ Nous aimerions) connaître le détail de l'ensemble des frais ( agence et notaire ) que vous voudrez bien joindre au compromis de vente.

Veuillez agréer, cher Monsieur Premont, l'expression de (mes \ nos) sentiments les meilleurs.

John et Mary Matthews

# Buy extra land when owner is not known

Sometimes you want to buy extra land and need to find out the owner. The original estate agent or the notaire should be able to get this under way for you.

25 The Groves
Winchester
Hampshire
WR7 9PP

22nd March, 2006

Monsieur G. PREMONT
Agent Immobilier
4 rue du Parc
75000 - PARIS

Dear Sirs,

**Le Petit Bois, 53756 Laval**

(I \ We) have recently bought the above property through yourselves and would like to purchase additional land as marked on the enclosed plan.

Could you establish the owner of the land and enquire if they would be interested in selling this to (me \ us) and at what price per sq metre?

(I \ We) would pay all surveyor and legal fees incurred.

As soon as you give an indication that they would be prepared to sell and we agree a price (I \ we) would ask that you instruct a surveyor to mark out the land and you commence the purchase.

Please advise me as to what moneys you required transferred to yourselves.

Yours faithfully

John and Janice Clewis

Change to grey box contents if letter is to a Notaire.

Select singular or plural from brackets.

Maître Laurence
Notaire
Place de Paris
76500 Montpellier

John et Janice Clewis
25 The Groves
Winchester
Hampshire
WR7 9PP

Winchester, le 22 mars 2006

Monsieur G. PREMONT
Agent Immobilier
4 rue du Parc
75000 – PARIS

Cher Monsieur,  ⟵  Cher Maître

Objet  Propriété sise à : Le Petit Bois, 53756 Laval

(J'ai \ Nous avons) acheté, par votre intermédiaire, la propriété citée ci-dessu et ( je voudrais \ nous voudrions) acquérir une parcelle supplémentaire dans le terrain joutant ma (notre) propriété.

Pourriez-vous contacter le propriétaire de ce terrain et lui demander s'il serait d'accord pour (m'en \ nous en) vendre une portion? - Dans l'affirmatif quel serait le prix du mètre carré?

Bien entendu, (je prends \ nous prenons) en charge les frais de délimitation et de l'acte.

Sitôt que vous aurez reçu une réponse affirmative pour cette cession et que nous aurons négocié surface et prix, voudriez-vous avoir l'obligeance de quérir un géomètre et faire préparer l'acte de vente?

Veuillez également (me \ nous) faire connaître le coût de votre intervention.

(Je vous remercie \ Nous vous remercions) à l'avance de votre assistance et (je vous prie \ nous vous prions d'agréer cher (Monsieur \ Maître), l'expression de (mes \ nos) sentiments les meilleurs.

John Clewis                                    Janice Clewis

14

# Buy extra Land – Owner Known

Need extra land? If you know the owner a simple approach may tempt them to sell

25 The Groves
Winchester
Hampshire
WR7 9PP

22nd March, 2006

Mrs Prett,
Le Grand Bois
53759 Laval

Dear Madam,

### **Le Petit Bois, 53756 Laval**

(I \ We) have recently bought the above property and would like to purchase additional land as marked on the enclosed plan.

Would you be interested in selling this to (me \ us) and at what price per sq metre?
(I \ We) would pay all surveyor and legal fees incurred.

As soon as you give an indication that you would be prepared to sell and we agree a price (I \ we) will instruct our notaire to commence the purchase.

Yours faithfully

Peter and Marion Francis

Change the (singular \ plural) as required.

Peter et Marion Francis
25 The Groves
Winchester
Hampshire
WR7 9PP

Winchester, le 22 mars 2006

Madame Prett,
Le Grand Bois
53759 Laval

**Objet : Propriété sise à : Le Petit Bois, 53756 Laval**

Chère Madame,

(J'ai \ Nous avons) acheté la propriété citée ci-dessus et (je voudrais \ nous voudrions) acquérir une parcelle supplémentaire dans le terrain joutant cette propriété.

Seriez-vous intéressée par cette cession à (mon \ notre) profit et quel serait le prix du mètre carré?

Bien entendu (je prends \ nous prenons) en charge les frais de géomètre et d'acte de vente.

Dans le cas où vous seriez d'accord sur cette cession et après négociation de la surface et du prix, voudriez-vous avoir l'obligeance de demander à notre notaire de préparer l'acte de vente?

(Je vous adresse \ Nous vous adressons) nos remerciements anticipés pour l'étude que vous voudrez bien faire de (ma \ notre) demande.

Veuillez accepter l'expression de (mes \ nos) sentiments les meilleurs.

Peter et Marion Francis

## Confirm Appointment and "bon de visite"

French estate agents ask all prospective clients to sign a bon de visite – this confirms that it was they who introduced the client and ensures their commis--sion payment.

25 The Groves
Winchester
Hampshire
WR7 9PP

22nd September, 2006

Monsieur G. PREMONT
Euro Immobilier
4 rue du Parc
75000 - PARIS

Dear Mr. PREMONT,

Thank you for arranging the appointments to view properties on 5th October 2006 at 10 a.m. (I \ We) confirm that (I \ we) will meet you at your office at that time.

(I \ We) (enclose the completed "Bon de Visite" as requested.\ will sign the "Bon de Visite" in your office, prior to viewing the properties.)

Yours faithfully,

John and Janice Clewis

Select the (singular \ plural) and the choice of sentence for the "Bon de visite"

John et Janice Clewis
25 The Groves
Winchester
Hampshire
WR7 9PP

Winchester le 22 septembre, 2006

> If this letter is to a
> notaire use "Maître"
> and "Office Notorial"

Monsieur G. PREMONT
Euro Immobilier
4 rue du Parc
75000 - PARIS

Cher (Monsieur \ Maître) PREMONT ,

(Je vous remercie \ Nous vous remercions ) d'avoir organisé les rendez-vous
pour la visite des propriétés le 5 Octobre 2006 à 10 heures du matin, et vous
(confirme \ confirmons ) que (je vous rencontrerai \ nous vous rencontrerons ) à
votre (Agence \ Office Notarial ) aux date et heure fixées.

Je joins \ Nous joignons ) à ce pli le " Bon de Visite " complété et signé.
Je désire \ Nous désirons ) signer ce " Bon de Visite " en votre Bureau , avant la
visite des propriétés .

> Select one of these sentences

En l'attente de vous rencontrer, veuillez agréer, cher Monsieur , l'expression de
(mes \ nos ) meilleurs sentiments.

John et Janice Clewis

18

# Insert Clause Suspensive in the Compromis de vente

These are just a few of the many clauses available. Only use the ones you need and take advice before signing any contract. You cannot add clauses once the compromis de vente has been signed.

25 The Groves
Winchester
Hampshire
WR7 9PP

22  Mars, 2006

Monsieur G. PREMONT
Agent Immobilier
4 rue du Parc
75000 – PARIS

Dear Sir

Thank you for sending the initial contract for Le Petit Bois, 53467 Laval.

(I \ We) would like the following suspension clauses to be inserted:

Mortgage offer for €120,000
Tontine for myself and my wife, Mrs Pauline Havers
Planning consents for renovations

When I receive the amended contract I (we) will sign the contract and return it immediately.


Yours faithfully,


John Havers

Remove unwanted clauses and ensure the correct form of address is chosen for estate agent or notaire. Mortgage figure shown is an example only.

John Havers
25 The Groves
Winchester
Hampshire
WR7 9PP

Winchester le 22 mars 2006

Maître Laurence                     Monsieur G. PREMONT
Notaire                             Agent Immobilier
Place de Paris                      4 rue du Parc
76500 Montpellier                   75000 – PARIS

Use this wording style if you are writing to a notaire

Cher (Monsieur \ Maître),

Je vous remercie de l'envoi du contrat initial concernant la propriété (Le Petit Bois, 53467 Laval).

(J'aimerais \ Nous aimerions) y insérer les conditions suspensives suivantes:

Emprunt hypothécaire pour la somme de 120000 Euros
Clause Tontine, à mon nom et à celui de ma femme, Mme Pauline Havers
Permis de construire pour des rénovations.

Quand je recevrai le contrat ainsi modifié (je vous le retournerai, \ nous vous retournerions,) signé, immédiatement.

Avec mes remerciements anticipés, je vous prie d'agréer, cher (Monsieur \ Maître), l'expression de mes meilleurs sentiments.

John Havers

## Sample Clause Suspensives

These are just a few of the common clauses and only legal advice will give you them all. They must be inserted in the initial contract and cannot be added after the Compromis de vente has been signed. Whatever the sales agent says, do not rush to sign until you are satisfied with the conditions.

Obtaining planning consents for construction or renovation.

Permission for minor changes

Obtain a satisfacory mortgage offer.

Sale of your house in UK    *(not likely to be accepted)*

Satisfactory building survey

Satisfactory wood and termite surveys

No known major development of the area.

The searches at the Land Registry relating to the property must not show any mortgage that is not fully covered by the sale price.

That any right of preemption is not exercised.

Existance of a certificat d'urbanisme

Restrictive clauses or prohibition of construction.

Select the clauses that you require or have been advised to insert

Obtention du permis de construire

Autorisation de travaux

Obtention d'un prêt hypothécaire

Vente de votre propriété en Angleterre

Etat satisfaisant de la construction (demande de certificat d'absence d'amiante)

Etat satisfaisant des charpentes et planchers en bois ( demande de certificat d'absence de termite )

Développement connu de la région  (industriel, bruyant, nuisible etc.)

Etat hypothécaire - Si oui , demander confirmation que cette hypothèque est bien  couverte par le prix de vente. (purge d'hypothèque )

Droit de préemption: public ou privé pouvant être exercé.
( délais de réponse )

Certificat d'Urbanisme

Clauses restrictives ou de non constructibilité.

# Change the Date for Completion

You may need to change the date of completion and, where there is good reason most vendors and notaires will be helpful.

25 The Groves
Winchester
Hampshire
WR7 9PP

22nd March, 2006

Maître Laurence
Notaire
Place de Paris
76500 Montpellier

Dear Sirs,

**<u>Grand Mers, St Lucent, 66543 Montpellier</u>**

You act on behalf of (myself \ ourselves) and the vendors for the purchase of the above property and you have advised us that signature of the Acte Authentique or Acte de Vente will be at 11am Monday the 6th January 2006.

Unfortunately (I \ we) are unable to be present for this date due to prior commitments and would ask that the date be changed to 15th March, 2006.

Please advise (me \ us) of the revised date as soon as possible.

Yours faithfully,

John and Janice Clewis

Change the (singular \ plural) as required.

John et Janice Clewis
25 The Groves
Winchester
Hampshire
WR7 9PP
United Kingdom

Winchester, le 22 mars 2006

Maître Laurence
Notaire
Place de Paris
76500 Montpellier

Cher Maître,

**Grand Mers, St Lucent, 66543 Montpellier**

Vous êtes (mon \ notre) intermédiaire auprès des vendeurs pour l'acquisition de la propriété ci-dessus référencée et (vous m'avez avisé \ nous avez avisés) que la signature de l'acte de vente ou acte authentique aurait lieu le lundi 6 janvier 2006 à 11 heures du matin.

Malheureusement, il (m'est \ nous est) impossible de (m'y \ nous y) présenter à cette date ayant (moi-même \ nous-mêmes) une obligation importante, aussi auriez-vous l'amabilité de bien vouloir reporter ce rendez-vous au 15 mars 2006.

Veuillez (me \ nous) faire savoir, par prochain courrier, si ce report de date vous convient. (Je vous en remercie \ Nous vous en remercions) bien vivement à l'avance.

Veuillez agréer, cher Maître, l'expression de (mes \ nos) meilleurs sentiments.

John et Janice Clewis

# Finalise date of contract

Sometimes the French system seems slow and a polite request for a completion date works. Change the dates to suit your arrangements

25 The Groves
Winchester
Hampshire
WR7 9PP

22nd March, 2006

Maître Laurence
Notaire
Place de Paris
76500 Montpellier

Dear Sirs,

### Grand Mers, St Lucent, 66543 Montpellier

You act on behalf of (myself \ ourselves) and the vendor(s) for the purchase of the above property.

(I \ We) are anxious to fix a completion date for this matter and would request the date for signature of the (Acte Authentique \ Acte de Vente) be fixed as soon as possible.

(I \ We) will be in France from 20\04\2006 to 30\04\2006 and would like the matter to be finalised during this period. Please advise (me \ us) of an appropriate date and time.

Yours faithfully,

John and Janice Clewis

Change the (singular \ plural) as required. Be realistic about the time frame you give – France just isn't as fast on contracts as you might like.

---

John et Janice Clewis
25 The Groves
Winchester
Hampshire
WR7 9PP
United Kingdom

Winchester, le 22 mars 2006

> Maître Laurence
> Notaire
> Place de Paris
> 76500 Montpellier

Cher Maître

## Grand Mers, St Lucent, 66543 Montpellier

Vous agissez comme intermédiaire entre (moi-même \ nous-mêmes) et (le vendeur \ les vendeurs) pour l'acquisition de cette propriété.

(Je vous demande \ Nous vous demandons) de préparer rapidement la rédaction du compromis de vente, de (m'en \ nous en) adresser une copie et de fixer une date définitive pour sa signature.

(Je viendrai \ Nous viendrons) en France entre le 20\04\2006 et le 30\04\2006 et (aimerais \ aimerions) finaliser cette opération lors de ce séjour. Veuillez (me \ nous) fixer le plus tôt possible la date et l'heure.

Avec (mes\ nos) remerciements anticipés, veuillez agréer, cher Maître, l'expression de (mes \ nos) sentiments les meilleurs.

John et Janice Clewis

# Search for Debts on Property

Unlike the U.K, debts of a former owner can be carried over when a property is sold in France and it is essential to make sure that all debts have been paid prior to completion.

25 The Groves
Winchester
Hampshire
WR7 9PP


22nd March, 2006

Maître Laurence
Notaire
Place de Paris
76500 Montpellier


Dear Sirs,

### Le Petit Bois - St Pierre de Ernee 53500


(I am \ We are) concerned that there may be existing debt or charges against this property and would ask that you have a search made of the appropriate records to ensure the property is debt free on transfer to (myself \ ourselves).

Please advise (me \ us) of the result of this search as soon as possible.


Yours faithfully,


Gérard and Marion Broughton

Just make the singular \ plural changes as required and make sure you change the address to that of the property you are purchasing

Gérard et Marion Broughton
25 The Groves
Winchester
Hampshire
WR7 9PP

Winchester, le 22 mars 2006

Maître Laurence
Notaire
Place de Paris
76500 Montpellier

Cher Maître,

### Le Petit Bois - St Pierre de Ernee 53500

(J'ai \ Nous avons) entendu dire que, peut-être, il existerait des dettes ou charges contre cette propriété et (je vous demande \ nous vous demandons) de (me\ nous) faire savoir si vous avez fait ou pouvez faire des recherches à ce sujet et éventuellement régler la situation avec les vendeurs afin que le transfert à (mon \ notre ) profit soit levé de toute hypothèque, dettes ou charges.

Veuillez avoir l'amabilité de (me \ nous) tenir au courant le plus tôt possible.

Avec (mes \ nos) remerciements anticipés,veuillez agréer, cher Maître, l'expression de (mes \ nos ) meilleurs sentiments.

Gérard et Marion Broughton

## Marriage Status Clause in Contract

A very delicate subject both personally and as regards tax and inheritance. Research the subject before using these clauses and take expert legal advice if necessary.

25 The Groves
Winchester
Hampshire
WR7 9PP

22nd March, 2006

Maître Laurence
Notaire
Place de Paris
76500 Montpellier

Dear Sir,

**<u>Le Petit Bois 53000 Changé</u>**

(I \ We) have been advised that we require the final purchase contract to have a Clause Tontine to be inserted.

(I \ We) have been advised that we require the final purchase contract to include the clause stating our relationship is (married \ cohabiting)

Please advise as to any documentation you may require to do this.

Yours faithfully

Gérard Broughton

Select the clause you require, but take care, a mistake could be very expensive!

---

Gérard Broughton
25 The Groves
Winchester
Hampshire
WR7 9PP

Winchester, le 22 mars 2006

> Maître Laurence
> Notaire
> Place de Paris
> 76500 Montpellier

Cher Maître

### Le Petit Bois 53000 Changé

(J'ai été \ Nous avons été) informés qu'une clause tontine devrait être insérée dans le contrat de vente de la propriété ci-dessus référencée.

(J'ai été \ Nous avons été) informés qu'une clause de situation ou lien de parenté (régime matrimonial \ pacte civil de solidarité) devrait être incluse dans l'acte de vente de la propriété ci-dessus.

Veuillez me faire parvenir toute documentation requise de cette demande.

Avec mes remerciements anticipés, veuillez agréer, cher Maître, l'expression de mes sentiments les meilleurs.


Gérard Broughton

---

## Set up Power of Attorney

Not all agents or notaires will accept a "Pouvoir" or Power of attorney. It is sometimes used for the signing of the Compromis de Vente but is not likely to be accepted for the final contract.

25 The Groves
Winchester
Hampshire
WR7 9PP

22nd March, 2006

Monsieur G. Blanc
Agent Immobilier
4 rue du Parc
75000 - PARIS

Dear Mr. Blanc,

(I am \ We are) sorry that you are unable to send the contract to the UK for signature.

(I \ We) have appointed Mr. Pierre Chevaux, Les Petits-Bois 53872 - LAVAL to sign on (my \ our) behalf and he is in possession of Power of Attorney documentation.

Please contact Mr. Chevaux as soon as possible to make arrangements for the contract signing.

Yours faithfully,

Gérard and Marion Broughton

Select the singular \ plural and insert the name of the person who will act for you in place of M. Pierre Chevaux.  Ensure that you enclose of copy of the Pouvoir document with this letter.

Gérard et Marion Broughton
25 The Groves
Winchester
Hampshire
WR7 9PP

Winchester, le 22 mars 2006

Monsieur G. Blanc
Agent Immobilier
4 rue du Parc
75000 - PARIS

Cher Monsieur Blanc,

(Je suis désolé \ Nous sommes désolés) que vous n'ayez pu (m'\ nous) adresser le contrat à signer en Angleterre.

(J'ai \ Nous avons) désigné M. Pierre Chevaux, Les Petits-Bois 53872 - LAVAL pour signer à (ma \ notre) place et il est en possession de la procuration officielle préparée par mon avocat.

Veuillez avoir l'obligeance de contacter M. Chevaux dans les meilleurs délais pour aménager un rendez-vous pour la signature dudit acte.

Avec (mes \ nos) remerciements anticipés, recevez , Monsieur, (mes \ nos) salutations distinguées.

Gérard et Marion Broughton

## Pouvoir - Power of Attorney

This is a typical pouvoir but you need to check with the immobilier or notaire that it is acceptable. Check with your notaire if your have any doubts.

---

# Pouvoir

We the undersigned :       **Monsieur John Frederick CLEWIS**
                           **Madame  Janice Elaine CLEWIS**

Residing at:               **25 The Groves, Winchester, Hampshire, WR7 9PP**

Give all authority to      **Monsieur Pierre Chevaux**
                           **Les Petits-Bois**
                           **53872 – LAVAL**

For the purpose to sign for my account and in my name the offer to buy and the compromise de vente with the agency       **PREMONT IMMOBILIER**
                           **4 rue du Parc   75000 – PARIS**

A house situated at  **La Chasse, Rue de Picot 66579 Montpellier**

At a price of **125,000 euros  (One hundred and twenty-five thousand euros )**

Signed in good faith and with authority

Signed at  **WINCHESTER, ENGLAND**
Dated  **25 March, 2006**

**John Frederick CLEWIS**                           **Janice Elaine CLEWIS**

---

If it is in bold it must be changed to your own details. The English version is a guide only and has no authority in France.

# Pouvoir

(Je soussigné\e
Nous soussignés):  **Monsieur John Frederick CLEWIS**
**Madame Janice Elaine CLEWIS**

Demeurant\s:  **25 The Groves, Winchester, Hampshire, WR7 9PP**

(Donne\ Donnons) tous pouvoirs à **Monsieur Pierre Chevaux**
**Les Petits-Bois**
**53872 – LAVAL**

Aux fins de signer pour (mon \ notre) compte et en (mon \ notre) nom l'offre d'acquisition et le compromis de vente à l'agence  **PREMONT IMMOBILIER**
**4 rue du Parc**
**75000 – PARIS**

D'une maison sise à **La Chasse, Rue de Picot 66579 Montpellier**

Au prix de 125000 euros (Cent vingt cinq mille euros acte en main).

Faire pour servir et valoir ce que de droit.

Fait à **WINCHESTER, ANGLETERRE**

Le 25 mars 2006

**John Frederick CLEWIS**　　　　　　　　**Janice Elaine CLEWIS**

## Payment of Deposit or Final Payment

Important to make sure payments are in place on time. Take care to change the name of the bank and relevant property address.

25 The Groves
Winchester
Hampshire
WR7 9PP

22nd March, 2006

Maître Laurence
Notaire
Place de Paris
76500 Montpellier

Dear Mr. Lawrence,

I enclose (a cheque drawn on the bank, Credit Agricole \ an English bank draft) for 12345 euros as payment of the (deposit \ balance due) on property: Les Petits Bois 53501 - LAVA L

Please advise me of receipt of this payment.

Yours faithfully,

Gérard Broughton

It's really important not to make mistakes here – It's your money at stake. All the options are in the same order in the English and French versions.

---

Gérard et Marion Broughton
25 The Groves
Winchester
Hampshire
WR7 9PP

Winchester, le 22 mars 2006

Maître Laurence
Notaire
Place de Paris
76500 Montpellier

Maître,

Veuillez trouver sous ce pli (un chèque tiré sur la banque Crédit Agricole \ une traite bancaire de banque anglaise) pour le réglement de la somme de 12345 euros à (titre de garantie \ comme solde de prix ) sur la propriété sise à  Les Petits Bois 53501 - LAVAL

Je vous serais reconnaissant de bien vouloir m'accuser réception de ce réglement.

Avec mes remerciements anticipés, je vous prie d'agréer, Maître, l'expression de mes meilleurs sentiments.

Gérard Broughton

---

## Mobile Phones

Mobile phones are a freely available in France as in the U.K. When buying just the chip, make sure that your phone is open for use with any manufacturer's chip and not locked on a single supplier.

John et Mary Matthews
Le Petit Bois
53567 Laval

2 May, 2006

The PhoneHouse
40 Rue Royale Angle rue du Chariot
Orleans 45000

Dear Sirs,

I require a (pay as you go \ contract) phone chip that is compatible with (Orange \ SFR \ O2 \ NRJ) phone system for use in my Motorola phone model T912.

If you are able to provide this please advise me of the cost and provide the appropriate paperwork.

Please supply me with a pay as you go mobile phone as advertised in Mayenne Courier on 12\10\2006

I require €20 credit with the phone.

Please supply me with a contract mobile phone as advertised in Mayenne Courier on 12\10\2006.

Please provide the appropriate paperwork and advise what identification is required.

Please supply €20 credit for a (SRF \ Orange \ mobicarte) mobile (and install it on this mobile).

Yours faithfully,

John Matthews

Select the paragraphs you require and insert the appropriate network and value required.

---

John et Mary Matthews
Le Petit Bois
53567 Laval

Laval, le 2 mai 2006

The PhoneHouse
40 Rue Royale Angle rue du Chariot
Orleans 45000

Messieurs,

Je recherche une carte électronique (sans abonnement \ avec forfait) pour téléphone mobile qui soit compatible avec (Orange \ SFR \ O2 \ NRJ) et utilisable pour mon appareil Motorola modèle T912.

Si vous pouvez me la fournir, ayez l'obligeance de m'en aviser, de m'en donner le coût et de préparer le contrat approprié.

Veuillez me fournir un téléphone mobile sans abonnement, identique à celui paru dans le Courrier de la Mayenne du 12\10\2006.
Je souhaiterais un crédit de 20 euros avec ce téléphone.

Veuillez me fournir un téléphone mobile avec forfait, identique à celui paru dans le Courrier de la Mayenne du 12\10\2006.
Pourriez-vous avoir l'amabilité de me faire parvenir la documentation nécessaire et m'informer des éventuelles pièces d'identité indispensables à un tel achat.

Veuillez me fournir un crédit de 20 euros pour mobiles (SFR \ Orange\ Mobicarte) et l'installer sur ce mobile.

Avec mes remerciements anticipés, veuillez agréer, Messieurs, l'expression de mes sentiments distingués.

John Matthews

Sim Card only

Pay as you go

Contract

Top up

# Move Gas or Electricity meter

French gas and electricity meters tend to be placed in very strange places. Fortunately  GDF and EDF are quite helpful in moving them.

Le Petit Bois
Laval 53567

2nd May, 2006

Électricité de France,
Rue de l'est
53500 LAVAL

Dear Sirs,

I would like the meter from which my (gas \ electricity) supply enters the house moved from it's present position to a new location as shown on the enclosed sketch plan.

I would prefer the new meter to be located outside the house.

Could you please arrange for a technician to look at the possibility of doing this and let me have an estimate for the work.

Yours faithfully,

John Matthews

Utility addresses can be found either at the Mairie or through yellow pages http:\\www.pagesjaunes.fr\pj.cgi?lang=en.

John Matthews
Le Petit Bois
Laval 53567

Laval, le 2 mai 2006

Électricité de France,
Rue de l'est
53500 LAVAL

Messieurs,

Je voudrais vous demander de bien vouloir déplacer le compteur (gaz \ électrique) alimentant ma maison de sa position actuelle au nouvel emplacement noté sur le schéma ci-inclus.

Je souhaiterais que le nouveau compteur (gaz \ électrique) soit placé en dehors de la maison.

Voudriez-vous avoir l'amabilité de demander à un technicien d'examiner si mon projet est réalisable et me faire connaître le coût de ce travail.

Avec mes remerciements anticipés, veuillez agréer, Messieurs, l'expression, de mes sentiments distingués.

John Matthews

## Move Telephone or Electricity Pole

Telephone and electricity poles can to be placed very close to houses and sometimes cry out to be moved. Fortunately  GDF and EDF are quite helpful in moving them.

Le Petit Bois<br>
Laval 53567

2nd May, 2006

France Telecom
5 rue du Général De Gaulle
53500 LAVAL

Dear Sirs,

I would like the supply pole from which my (telephone \ electricity) supply enter the house moved from it's present position to a new location as shown on the enclosed sketch plan.

I  would prefer the new supply to the house to be installed underground.

Could you please arrange for a technician to look at the possibility of doing this and let me have an estimate for the work.

Yours faithfully,

John Matthews

Utility addresses can be found either at the Mairie or through yellow pages
http:\\www.pagesjaunes.fr\pj.cgi?lang=en.

John Matthews
Le Petit Bois
Laval 53567


Laval, le 2 mai 2006


                                        Électricité de France,
                                        Rue du Général de Gaulle
                                        53500 LAVAL


Messieurs,


Je vous serais obligé, si cela est possible, de déplacer le poteau portant la ligne
(téléphonique \ électrique) alimentant ma maison de son emplacement actuel à
celui noté sur le plan ci-inclus.

Je préfère que le nouveau branchement (téléphonique \ électrique) pour alimenter
ma maison soit souterrain.

Voudriez-vous avoir l'amabilité de demander à un technicien d'examiner si mon
projet est recevable et me faire connaître le coût de ce travail.

Avec mes remerciements anticipés, veuillez agréer, Messieurs, l'expression de
mes sentiments distingués.


John Matthews

## Redirect Your Post

Get the form from any "La Poste" office, complete it and have your mail redirected to another address in France of the UK.

Les Petits Bois
53501 - LAVAL

22nd August, 2006

The Manager,
La Poste,
Rue de Ville Blanche
53500 - LAVAL

Dear sir,

**1** Would you please send me a copy of the form to have my post redirected.

**2** Please find enclosed completed form, together with payment of €25 for redirection of my mail for a period of 6 months.

Yours faithfully,

Gérard Broughton

Select the paragraph to obtain the form or submit the form as needed.
The paragraphs are in the same numbered order for both languages.

Gérard et Marion BROUGHTON
Les Petits Bois
53501 - LAVAL

Laval, le 22 août 2006

Le directeur,
La Poste,
Rue de Ville Blanche
53500 – LAVAL

Monsieur le Directeur,

Veuillez avoir l'obligeance de m'adresser une formule pour me permettre de faire suivre mon courrier.

**1**

Veuillez trouver sous ce pli le formulaire complété avec réglement de 25€ pour faire suivre mon courrier durant une période de 6 mois.

**2**

Avec mes remerciements anticipés, veuillez agréer, Monsieur le Directeur, l'expression de mes sentiments distingués.

Gérard Broughton

## Temporary Electricity Supply

Look up the address for utilities in the phone book for the nearest large town.

Les Petits Bois
53501 - LAVAL

22nd August, 2006

EDF
118 rue Victor BOISSEL
53500 LAVAL

Dear Sirs,

**Les Petits Bois, 53501 - LAVAL**

(I \ We)would like to arrange for a temporary electricity supply to be connected to the above property to enable renovation work to commence.

Your estimate for cost and a date this can be done would be appreciated.

Yours faithfully,

Gérard and Marion Broughton

It may be possible to get a temporary supply during the period of renovation work. Make sure to get the correct address of the supply required and remember the singular \ plural choices.

---

Gérard et Marion Broughton
Les Petits Bois
53501 - LAVAL

Laval, le 22 août 2006

EDF
Rue de Marcel
53500 LAVAL

Monsieur le Directeur,

### Les Petits Bois, 53501 - LAVAL

(Je vous saurais grè \ Nous vous saurions grès) d'approvisionner temporairement en courant électrique la propriété ci-dessus référencée pour permettre le commencement des travaux.

Veuillez avoir l'amabilité de (me \ nous) tenir (informé \ informés) du coût de cet approvisionnement et de la date de fourniture .

Avec (mes \ nos) remerciements anticipés, veuillez agréer, Monsieur le Directeur l'expression de (mes \ nos) sentiments distingués.

Gérard et Marion Broughton

## Temporary Water Supply

Look up the address for utilities in the phone book for the nearest large town.

Les Petits Bois
53501 - LAVAL

22nd August, 2006

Service Municipal Eau et Assainissement
place du 11 Novembre
53000 LAVAL

Dear Sirs,

### Les Petits Bois, 53501 - LAVAL

Would you please arrange for a temporary Water supply to be connected to the above property to enable renovation work to commence.

Your estimate for cost and a date this can be done would be appreciated.

Yours faithfully,

Marion Broughton

It may be possible to get a temporary water supply during the period of renovation work. Make sure to get the correct address of the supply required and remember the singular \ plural choices.

---

Gérard et Marion Broughton
Les Petits Bois
53501 - LAVAL

Laval, le 22 août 2006

> Service Municipal Eau et Assainissement
> place du 11 Novembre
> 53000 LAVAL

Monsieur le Directeur,

### Les Petits Bois, 53501 - LAVAL

Je vous serais reconnaissant de bien vouloir prévoir un branchement provisoire à l'adduction d'eau pour permettre l'exécution des travaux envisagés dans la propriété citée en référence.

Ayez l'amabilité de me faire connaître le coût et la date de ce branchement.

Avec mes remerciements anticipés, veuillez agréer, Monsieur, l'expression de mes sentiments distingués.

Marion Broughton

---

## Transfer Utilities

All of the addresses can be found in pages jaunes or from the local mairie.

25 The Groves<br>
Winchester<br>
Hampshire<br>
WR7 9PP

22nd March, 2006

EDF GDF Services en Mayenne
35Bis rue Crossardière
53000 LAVAL

Dear Sirs,

**<u>Le Petit Bois,  Rue de Montagne, 53000 Laval</u>**

(I \ We) are purchasing the above property and would like the  (electricity \ gas \ water \ telephone) account to be transferred to (myself \ourselves).

(I \ We) enclose proof of ownership and would ask that this be done without delay.

Please send the appropriate forms and forms to enable the payment to be made by bankers order.

Yours faithfully,

Gérard and Marion Broughton

Lots of opportunities to make mistakes – careful with the singular \ plural choice and make sure you select the right utility. Addresses from the Mairie or pages jaune.

Gérard et Marion Broughton
25 The Groves
Winchester
Hampshire
WR7 9PP

Winchester, le 22 mars 2006

EDF GDF Services en Mayenne
Direction départementale
35Bis r Crossardière 53000 LAVAL

Messieurs,

**Le Petit Bois,  Rue de la Montagne, 53000 Laval**

(J'ai acheté \ Nous avons acheté) cette propriété et (je voudrais\ nous voudrions ) que les branchements (d'électricité \ de gaz \ d'eau \ de téléphone ) soient transférés à (mon \ notre ) nom.

(Je joins \ Nous joignons) à ce pli le certificat de propriété et vous demande de (me \ nous) faire connaître dans quel délai ce transfert pourra être effectué.

Veuillez (me \ nous) faire parvenir les formulaires adéquats pour que (je puisse\ nous puissions) en effectuer le réglement par ordre bancaire.

Avec (mes \ nos) remerciements anticipés, veuillez agréer, Messieurs, l'expression de (mes \ nos) sentiments distingués.

Gérard et Marion Broughton

## Install New Utilities

If you require installation of utility supplies from new you need to contact the supplying organisation. New installations may require a survey and an estimated costing.

25 The Groves
Winchester
Hampshire
WR7 9PP

22nd March, 2006

EDF GDF Services en Mayenne
35Bis, r Crossardière
53000 LAVAL


Dear Sirs,

**Le Petit Bois,  Rue de Montagne, 53000 Laval**


Would you please arrange for installation of a (telephone \water \ gas \ electrity) supply to this address.  Access to the property will be available from 21\05\2006. Kindly advise (me\ us) of the installation date and the cost of installation.


(I \ We) would like to pay by direct debit and would appreciate the appropriate forms.


Yours faithfully,



Gérard and Marion Broughton

Four letters in one – select the service you want connected and get the correct address for the utility. Pages jaunes or the mairie will provide this information.

Gérard et Marion Broughton
25 The Groves
Winchester
Hampshire
WR7 9PP

Winchester, le 22 mars 2006
EDF GDF Services en Mayenne
Direction départementale
35Bis, r Crossardière 53000 LAVAL

Messieurs,

### Le Petit Bois,  Rue de  la Montagne, 53000 Laval

(Je vous serais reconnaissante \ Nous vous serions reconnaissantes)  de bien vouloir envisager le branchement du téléphone à l'adresse ci-dessus. L'accès à cette propriété sera possible à compter du 21\05\2006. Veuillez avoir l'amabilité de (m'aviser \ nous aviser) de la date de ce branchement et de son coût.

Veuillez avoir l'amabilité d'effectuer le branchement, en eau potable, de la propriété citée en référence. L'accès à cette propriété sera possible à compter du 21\05\2006. Veuillez, s'il vous plaît, (m'aviser \ nous aviser) de la date de ce branchement et de son coût.

(Je vous serais reconnaissante \ Nous vous serions reconnaissante) de bien vouloir envisager le branchement du gaz de ville à l'adresse ci-dessus. L'accès à cette propriété sera possible à compter du 21\05\2006. Veuillez avoir l'amabilité de (m'aviser \ nous aviser) de la date de ce branchement et de son coût.

(Je vous serais reconnaissante \ Nous vous serions reconnaissante) de bien vouloir envisager l'installation de l'électricité à l'adresse ci-dessus. L'accès à cette propriété sera possible à compter du 21\05\2006. Veuillez avoir l'amabilité de (m'aviser \ nous aviser) de la date de cette installation et de son coût.

(Je désire \ Nous désirons) régler cette facture directement et celles des consommations également  - par virements automatiques et mensuellement  - et (vous demande \ vous demandons de (m'adresser \ nous adresser) le formulaire adéquat pour ce mode de réglement.

Avec (mes \ nos) remerciements anticipés,veuillez agréer, Messieurs, l'expression de (mes \ nos ) sentiments distingués.

Gérard et Marion Broughton

Phone

Water

Gas

Electricity

## TV Licence not Required

France tends to assume you have a TV and it requires licencing and you may well receive a demand for payment. If you have one then pay up - if you don't, then use this letter and return it to the address on the form.

Le Petit Bois
Laval 53567

2 May, 2006

Centre Régional de la Redevance,
Rue de Premier
53456 LAVAL

Dear Sirs,

**Television Licence at: Le Petit Bois, Laval 53567**

(I \ We) have received your letter regarding the need to have a television licence for the above property.

(I \ We) do not have a television installed or portable or video at this address and therefore a licence is not required.

Yours faithfully,

John Matthews

Change the address for your house and the return address for the form and send it off. The only excuse for not having a licence is not to have a television. Unlike the UK you cannot have a set and just watch videos or DVDs on it, you will still need a licence. From 2006 the licence fee is collected with taxe d'habitation.

John Matthews
Le Petit Bois
Laval 53567

Laval le 2 mai, 2006

Centre Régional de la Redevance,
Rue de Premier
53456 LAVAL

Messieurs,

**Redevance audiovisuelle à Le Petit Bois, Laval 53567**

(J'ai \ Nous avons) reçu votre courrier concernant la redevance audiovisuelle pour cette propriété.

(Je n'ai \ Nous n'avons) pas de télévision installée ou portable ou vidéo et par conséquent (je n'ai \ nous n'avons) pas de redevance à payer.

Avec (mes \ nos) sentiments distingués.

John Matthews

# Return goods under guarantee

You have as many consumer rights in France as the U.K. Make sure you have the receipt for the purchase. Often this is the only form of guarantee paperwork.

Les Petits Bois
53501 - LAVAL

22nd August, 2006

Hyper-U
Rte de Laval
53500 Mayenne

Dear Sirs,

**<u>Name of item Model Number and serial number</u>**

I purchased the above item at Hyper-U supermarket, Mayenne on 12\01\2006 and I am returning it to your company for repair or replacement under guarantee.

Proof of purchase is attached.

Yours faithfully,

Marion Broughton

Make sure to correctly identify the model and serial numbers and change the purchase location and date as needed.

---

Gérard et Marion BROUGHTON
Les Petits Bois
53501 - LAVAL

Laval, le 22 août 2006

Hyper U
Rte de Laval
53500 Mayenne

Monsieur,

### *Nom de l'article - No du modèle - et No de la série*

J'ai acheté l'article ci-dessus référencé au supermarché Hyper-U de Mayenne le 12\01\2006 et je l'ai renvoyé à votre compagnie pour sa réparation ou son remplacement sous garantie.

Sous ce pli, je joins le ticket d'achat.

Votre bien dévoué.

Marion Broughton

---

# Woodworm and Termite Survey

Old properties are beautiful to look at but few escape the ravages of wood infestation in some form. If you aren't sure about how to treat timber in your house talk to an expert.

25 The Groves
Winchester
Hampshire
WR7 9PP

22nd March, 2006

Charpenet (SARL)
60 rue Champ de Foire
53140 Pré en Pail

Dear Sirs,

### Le Petit Bois 53000 Changé

I require an independent survey for wood decay, insect infestation and termites for the above property.

Please advise as to your charges, if any, for this and the date you will be able to undertake the survey.

The survey should be sent to myself: Mr Broughton , 25 The Groves, Winchester, Hampshire. WR7 9PP England.

Yours faithfully

Gérard Broughton

The name and address of the property to be checked has to be changed together with the address the survey is to be sent to.

---

Gérard Broughton
25 The Groves
Winchester
Hampshire
WR7 9PP

Winchester, le 22 mars 2006

Charpenet (SARL)
60 rue Champ de Foire
53140 Pré en Pail

Messieurs,

### Le Petit Bois 53000 Changé

Je voudrais une expertise spécifique concernant l'état des charpentes, planchers et autres bois...au niveau de pourriture, attaques de termites ou de vers en ma propriété citée en référence.

Veuillez me faire savoir si cette expertise est de votre compétence et si oui, à quelle date vous pourrez l'établir.

Le résultat de cette expertise pourra m'être adressé à: Mr Broughton, 25 The Groves, Winchester, Hampshire.WR7 9PP Angleterre.

Avec mes remerciements anticipés, veuillez agréer, Messieurs, l'expression de mes sentiments distingués.

Gérard Broughton

---

## Arrange survey for Fosse Septique

Surveys for fosse septiques can only be done by approved companies – your local mairie will give you a list.

Le Petit Bois
53567 Laval

2nd May 2006

SERPA
Rue des Fosses
LAVAL
53300 - LAVAL

Dear Sirs

### Property: Le Petit Bois, St Hillaire, 53509 Laval

(I \ We) have been given your name by the Mairie at Laval as being approved to carry out surveys for a fosse septique.

Would you please confirm your fees and a date that the survey can be carried out.

Please advise as to the time between the survey and receipt of the survey by (myself \ ourselves).

Yours faithfully,

Frederick and Sandra Picard

Make the (singular \ plural) changes and remember to insert the correct town whose mairie supplied the contractors name.

---

Frederick et Sandra Picard
Le Petit Bois
53567 Laval

Laval, le 2 mai 2006

SERPA
Rue des Fosses
LAVAL
53300 - LAVAL

Monsieur,

**Objet: Le Petit Bois, St Hillaire, 53509 Laval**

(J'ai \ Nous avons) eu votre nom par la Mairie de Laval qui a approuvé l'étude de la mise en place d'une fosse septique sur la propriété citée en référence.

Veuillez avoir l'obligeance de (me \ nous) faire connaître le coût de cette étude et la date de réalisation.
Avec (mes \ nos) remerciements anticipés, veuillez agréer, Monsieur, l'expression de (mes \ nos) meilleurs sentiments.

Frederick et Sandra Picard

---

## Instruct a Surveyor

Three of the most commonly required services from the surveyor. Make sure to establish the fees in advance – they are often from a standard range with very high minimums.

25 The Groves
Winchester
Hampshire
WR7 9PP

22nd March, 2006

Cabinet Zubber
58 Rue de Val de Mayenne
53500 - LAVAL

Dear Sirs

### Re Property: Les Petit Bois, 53500 Laval

**1** (I \ We) require a plan masse for the above property for a planning application. Would you please advise (me \ us) as to the cost and time required for this.

**2** (I \ We) require a full structural survey on the above property . Would you please advise (me \ us) as to the cost and time required for this.

**3** (I \ We) require a survey of boundaries of the above property . Would you please advise (me \ us) as to the cost and time required for this.

Yours faithfully,

Gérard and Marion Broughton

Select the service you require and delete the other numbered paragraphs. They are in the same order for English and French.

Gérard et Marion Broughton
25 The Groves
Winchester
Hampshire
WR7 9PP

Winchester, le 22 mars 2006

Cabinet Zubber
58 Rue du Val de Mayenne
53500 - LAVAL

Monsieur,

### Les Petit Bois, 53500 Laval

(J'aimerais \ Nous aimerions) que vous nous adressiez un plan de masse de la propriété citée en référence pour un projet en cours d'étude. | 1 |

(J'aimerais \ Nous aimerions) que vous nous fassiez un levé de terrain complet de la propriété citée en référence. | 2 |

(J'aimerais \ Nous aimerions) que vous nous fixiez les limites exactes de la propriété citée en référence. | 3 |

Voudriez avoir l'amabilité de (m'en \ nous en) donner le coût et de (me \ nous) dire quand vous pourrez adresser ce plan?

Avec (mes \ nos) remerciements anticipés pour votre réponse rapide, veuillez agréer, Monsieur, l'expression de (mes \ nos) meilleurs sentiments.

Gérard et Marion Broughton

# Certificat d' urbanisme

It is essential that you establish the existence of a certificat d' urbanisme and if it isn't produced by the vendor ask for it.

25 The Groves
Winchester
Hampshire
WR7 9PP

22nd March, 2006

Monsieur G. PREMONT
Agent Immobilier
4 rue du Parc
75000 - PARIS

Dear Sirs

**<u>Le Petit Bois, Montpellier  65789</u>**

Thank you for your help in the proposed purchase of the above property

Would you please confirm that the property has a certificat d'urbanisme.

Your assistance in this matter would be greatly appreciated.

Yours faithfully,

John  and Janice Clewis

John et Janice Clewis
25 The Groves
Winchester
Hampshire
WR7 9PP

Winchester, le 22 mars 2006

Monsieur G. PREMONT
Agent Immobilier
4 rue du Parc
75000 - PARIS


Monsieur,

**OBJET : Le Petit Bois, Montpellier  65789**


(Je vous remercie \ Nous vous remercions) beaucoup de votre intervention relative à la proposition d'acquisition de la propriété citée en référence.

Voudriez-vous confirmer que le certificat d'urbanisme de cette propriété est conforme à la réglementation et m'en faire parvenir une copie?

Votre aide à ce sujet sera très appréciée et (je vous remercie \ nous vous remercions) vivement de votre prochaine réponse.

Veuillez recevoir, Monsieur, l'expression de (mes \ nos) meilleurs sentiments.


John et Janice Clewis

# Get Forms for Planning application

**Permis de Construire** for new construction or major renovation or conversion.
**Autorisation de Travaux** for new windows or similar small projects.

Le Petit Bois
53000
CHANGE

10<sup>th</sup> October 2006

The Mayor of Changé
La Mairie
53000 – CHANGE

Dear Mr Mayor,

### Le Petit Bois 53000 Changé

I propose to apply for (planning consent \ permission for work) and I would appreciate the appropriate number of forms to enable an application to be submitted. I will call at your Mairie during my next visit to France on 28\10\2006.

If you have any literature describing the application procedure and documentation I would appreciate a copy of it.

Yours faithfully

Jason Harmers

Select the forms required for the project you want.

---

Jason Harmers
Le Petit Bois
53000
CHANGÉ

Changé le 10 octobre 2006

Monsieur le Maire de Changé
La Mairie
53000 - CHANGÉ

Monsieur le Maire,

### Le Petit Bois 53000 Changé

J'ai l'intention de faire une demande ( de permis de construire \ d'autorisation de travaux ) et vous serais reconnaissant de vouloir bien me faire connaître le nombre de formules appropriées, de me les adresser ou me dire si je peux les récupérer en votre Mairie lors de ma prochaine visite en France, vers le 28\10\2006.

Je serais heureux, également, d'avoir une documentation sur la procédure à suivre en la matière.

Je vous remercie bien vivement à l'avance de la réponse que vous voudrez bien me faire, et vous prie d'agréer, Monsieur le Maire, l'expression de mes meilleurs sentiments.

Jason Harmers

# Object to proposed Planning permission

Objections must be environmental, privacy, non compliance with regulations or safety orientated. I don't like the idea or the owner is not a valid ground! The above are guidelines only and not guaranteed objections.

Les Petits Bois
53501 - LAVAL

22nd August, 2006

Mairie de Laval
Place du 11 Novembre
53013 LAVAL Cedex

Dear Mr Mayor,

### Permis de Construire No: 231\AY23\472006

(I \ We) wish to lodge a formal objection to the above application based on the following (reason \ reasons):

**1** The proposed building will overlook my property and remove privacy for my family.

**2** The proposed building is not in keeping with existing building of the area.

**3** The area is a conservation area and proposals are inappropriate.

**4** The proposal will increase traffic to a dangerous level.

Yours faithfully,

Gérard and Marion Broughton

Change the singular \ plural as required.

These are a few of the standard objections but you must convey any special objections.

---

Gérard et Marion BROUGHTON
Les Petits Bois
53501 - LAVAL


Laval, le 22 août 2006

> Mairie de Laval
> Place du 11 Novembre
> 53013 LAVAL Cedex


Monsieur le Maire,

### Demande de Permis de construire No: 231\AY23\472006

(Je désire \ Nous désirons) porter une objection formelle au projet faisant l'objet du permis de construire ci-dessus pour (le motif suivant \ les motifs suivants):

La contruction prévoit une vue sur ma propriété et ôte ainsi toute intimité à ma famille. **1**

Le projet n'est pas en harmonie avec les contructions du secteur. **2**

Le secteur est une zone protégée et la construction proposée est inappropriée. **3**

Le projet tend à accroître la circulation à un niveau dangereux. **4**


Avec l'espoir que ma requête sera examinée avec toute l'attention désirée, (je vous prie \ nous vous prions) d'agréer, Monsieur le Maire, l'expression de (mes \ nos) sentiments les meilleurs.


Gérard et Marion BROUGHTON

# Submit Permis de Construire

The list of documents is that which is generally required. You will need to establish from the planning department at the Mairie of any additional requirements. This may vary from region to region.

25 The Groves
Winchester
Hampshire
WR7 9PP

22nd March, 2006

Monsieur le Maire de Changé
53000 – CHANGE


Dear Mr Mayor,

### Le Petit Bois 53000 Changé

(I \ We)enclose completed permis de construire forms and the following documents.

**Plans to scale:**
Front Rear and sides of property.
Floor plan prior to proposed work
Floor plan ground and first floor, showing proposed alterations
Plan Masse (prior to proposed extension)
Plan Masse (showing proposed extension)
Plan of area

**Photographs**
Close up and distance of front and rear of property

**Descriptive Notice**


Yours faithfully



Gérard and Marion Broughton

Make sure to include all of the documents, plans, photos and environmental statement require to accompany the application.

---

Gérard et Marion Broughton
25 The Groves
Winchester
Hampshire
WR7 9PP

Winchester, le 22 mars 2006

Monsieur le Maire de Changé
53000 – CHANGE

Monsieur le Maire,

### Le Petit Bois 53000 Changé

(Je vous prie \ Nous vous prions) de vouloir bien trouver sous ce pli la demande de permis de construire remplie et dûment datée et signée ainsi que les pièces s'y rattachant. A savoir:

*Plans à l'échelle*
    Façade, arrière-façade et pignons de la construction
    Plan rez-de-chaussée avant travaux
    Plan rez-de-chaussée et étage montrant les travaux d'aménagement.
    Plan de masse avant extension
    Plan de masse montrant les travaux d'extension
    Plan de situation

*Photos*
    Vue en gros plan et à distance des façades arrière et avant de la propriété.

*Notice descriptive*

Avec mes remerciements anticipés pour la bonne suite que vous voudrez bien apporter à ce dossier, veuillez agréer, Monsieur le Maire, l'expression de (mes \ nos) meilleurs sentiments.

Gérard et Marion Broughton

---

## Submit Permis de Travaux

A much simpler application than full planning permission and the list of documents is much shorter.

---

25 The Groves
Winchester
Hampshire
WR7 9PP

22nd March, 2006

Monsieur le Maire de Changé
53000 – CHANGE

Dear Mr Mayor,

### <u>Le Petit Bois 53000 Changé</u>

(I \ We) enclose completed Permis de Travaux forms and the following documents.

**Plans to scale:**

Plan Masse (Outline plan of property and boundaries **prior** to proposed extension)
Plan Masse (Outline plan of property and boundaries **showing** proposed extension)
Elevations of property affected by alterations

**Photographs**
Several photographs of elevations affected by proposed alterations

Yours faithfully

Gérard and Marion Broughton

---

Make sure to include all of the documents, plans, photos and environmental statement require to accompany the application.

---

Gérard et Marion Broughton
25 The Groves
Winchester
Hampshire
WR7 9PP

Winchester, le 22 mars 2006

> Monsieur le Maire de Changé
> 53000 – CHANGÉ

Monsieur le Maire,

### **Le Petit Bois 53000 Changé**

Veuillez bien trouver sous ce pli le dossier de permis de travaux complété, daté et signé, accompagné des document suivants:

*Plans à l'échelle*

> Plan de masse indiquant le périmètre de la maison et limites antérieures à l'extension.
> Plan de masse indiquant l'extension prévue.
> Plan d'élevation portant les modifications envisagées.

*Photos*
> Plusieurs photos des élévations affectées par les modifications envisagées.

Avec (mes \ nos) remerciements anticipés pour la bonne suite que vous voudrez bien apporter à ce dossier, veuillez agréer, Monsieur le Maire, l'expression de (mes \ nos) meilleurs sentiments.

Gérard et Marion Broughton

---

## Opening Bank Accounts

Take this letter to the bank of your choice together with the necessary documents. You need to be there in person to sign the appropriate forms. An account can be opened with a nominal sum.

Les Petits Bois
53501 - LAVAL


22nd August, 2006


Crédit Agricole
34, avenue Pierre Semard
95400 Arnouville les Gonesse


Dear Sirs,

(I \ We) wish to open a current account with cheque book and bankers card.

**1** (My \ Our) passports and proof of ownership of property are enclosed.


**2** (I \ We) wish to open a savings account with an opening deposit of €500.

(My \ Our) current account is No:12345\FR\0167


**3** (My \ Our) current account is No:12345\FR\0167 . (I \ We) wish to have a debit card for use with this account.

**4** (I \ We) wish to open an account for chèque d'emploi.

(My \ Our) current account is No:12345\FR\0167


Yours faithfully,


Gérard and Marion Broughton

As well as the singular \ plural choices you need to select the paragraph appropriate to your needs

Gérard et Marion BROUGHTON
Les Petits Bois
53501 - LAVAL

Laval, le 22 août 2006

Crédit Agricole
34, avenue Pierre Semard
95400 Arnouville les Gonesse

Monsieur le Directeur,

(Je voudrais \ Nous voudrions ouvrir un compte courant à votre Banque et obtenir un carnet de chèque ainsi qu'une carte bancaire.

(Mon \ Ma \ Nos) passeport(s) et le certificat de propriété sont joints à ce pli.

1

(Je voudrais \ Nous Voudrions) ouvrir un livret d'épargne ou similaire avec un dépôt d'ouverture de 500€.

(Mon \ Notre) compte courant est No: 12345\FR\0167.

2

(Mon \ Notre) compte courant est No: 12345\FR\0167. (Je voudrais \ Nous voudrions) recevoir une carte bancaire pour utiliser ce compte.

3

(Je voudrais \ Nous voudrions ouvrir un compte Chèque d'emploi.

(Mon \ Notre) compte courant est No: 12345\FR\0167.

4

Avec (mes \ nos) remerciements anticipés pour votre réponse, veuillez agréer, Monsieur le Directeur, l'expression de (mes \ nos) sentiments distingués.

Gérard et Marion Broughton

# Change address at the Bank

Your account number and address of the bank can be found on your cheque book or statement.

Le Petit Bois
67879 Limoge

3rd December 2006

Crédit Agricole
34 avenue Pierre Semard
95400 Arnouville les Gonesse

Dear Sirs,

**<u>Account No:12345\FR\0167</u>**

(I \ We) wish to change address details for the above account to those shown below:

BLANNIN  Joseph and Marie
Le Petit Bois
67879 Limoge

Please advise (me \ us) when this has been done.

Yours faithfully,

Joseph and Marie Blannin

Just fill in the account number change the address and delete the (male \ female) as required.

---

Joseph et Marie BLANNIN
Le Petit Bois
67879 Limoges

Limoges, le 3 décembre 2006

Crédit Agricole
34 avenue Pierre Semard
95400 Arnouville les Gonesse

Monsieur,

**_Objet :_ Compte No:12345\FR\0167**

(Je désire \ Nous désirons) modifier l'adresse du compte cité en référence comme suit:

Joseph et Marie Blannin
Le Petit Bois
67879 Limoges

Ayez l'obligeance de (me \ nous) prévenir lorsque cette modification sera effectuée.

Avec (mes \ nos) remerciements anticipés,veuillez agréer, Monsieur, l'expression de (mes \ nos ) sentiments les meilleurs.

Joseph et Marie Blannin

## Confirmation of Payment and Send Cheque

French bureaucracy often mislays payment and it is wise to query any reminders you receive.

---

Grand Mers
St Lucent
66543 Montpellier

23rd October, 2006

Jacques Perrier,
Maçon,
53509 St Hilare.

**Invoice: 3457\BYT**

Dear Sirs

> Query payment has been received

Your account for €543 was paid by cheque drawn on the bank Credit Agricole on 20th September, 2006. I have not received a receipt from you and would ask that you confirm payment has been received.

> Send cheque in payment of invoice

Please find enclosed a cheque for 543 euros in payment of invoice 3457\BYT. I would ask for confirmation of receipt of this payment.

Yours faithfully,

James Peterson

---

Just change the addresses, payment amount, invoice reference and dates to your requirements and delete the unwanted paragraph.

James Peterson
Grand Mers
 St Lucent
66543 Montpellier

Montpellier, le 23 octobre 2006

Jacques Perrier
Maçon,
53509 St Hilare.

**Objet: Facture 3457\BYT**

Monsieur,

Je vous ai réglé l'acompte demandé de 543 euros par chèque bancaire tiré sur la banque Crédit Agricole le 20 septembre 2006 - Vous ne m'en avez pas adressé quittance.

Veillez trouver ci-joint ce chèque de 543 euros en reglement de facture 3547\BYT.

Veuillez avoir l'obligeance de me confirmer que vous avez bien reçu ce chèque.

Recevez mes remerciements anticipés et mes meilleurs sentiments.

James Peterson

Query payment

Send chèque

## Get Bank details for Telegraphic Transfer

Not everybody you deal with will automatically give you the correct details to enable a swift telegraphic transfer of money. Don't forget the (singular \ plural) choice.

Les Petits-Bois
53872 - LAVAL


12<sup>th</sup> April, 2006


Maître Laurence
Notaire
Place de Paris
76500 Montpellier



Dear Sir,

(I \ We) wish to make payment for (deposit \ property payment) by telegraphic transfer from my UK bank account.

Please send (me \ us) details by (post \ e-mail) of your IBAN account number, the name of the account holder and the name and address of the bank to be used.


Yours faithfully,



Gerald Clements

Just select the choices you require which are in the same order as the English version

---

Gerald Clements
Les Petits-Bois
53872 - LAVAL

Laval, le 12 avril 2006

> Maître Laurence
> Notaire
> Place de Paris
> 76500 Montpellier

Cher Maître,

(Je voudrais \ Nous voudrions faire un virement en paiement d'un (acompte sur prix d'achat \ prix d'achat de propriété) par transfert télégraphique de (mon \ notre) compte bancaire en Angleterre.

Veuillez avoir l'obligeance de (me \ nous) faire connaître le détail du relevé d'identité bancaire du détenteur du compte auquel (je dois\ nous devons) faire exécuter ce virement ainsi que de (m' \ nous) adresser ce RIB par (courrier \ par e-mail) à l'adresse suivante:

Avec (mes \ nos) remerciements anticipés, veuillez agréer, Monsieur, l'expression de (mes \ nos) meilleurs sentiments.

Gerald Clements

---

# Arrange Telegraphic Transfer

All of the French details can be found in your French cheque book on the R.I.B. page.

---

Le Petit Bois<br>
67879 Limoges

3rd December 2006

Crédit Agricole
34, avenue Pierre Semard
95400 Arnouville les Gonesse

Dear Sirs,

### *Objet :* Compte No:12345\FR\0167

I wish to make an inter bank telegraphic transfer from the above account to the payee shown below:

Mr Joe Clements
Account No: 23456789  sort code: 00-00-01
Postal Address: (M. Clements)
Bank Name:
Full postal address of bank
Town
Postcode
Iban No:

Date transfer to be made.
Currency to be used: Euro (£ sterling) (other)

Please advise me when this has been done.

Yours faithfully,

Marie Blannin

Just fill in the account number and other details and change the name as required. They are in the same order for English and French letters.

Joseph et Marie Blannin
Le Petit Bois
67879 Limoges

Limoges, le 3 décembre 2006

Crédit Agricole
34, avenue Pierre Semard
95400 ARNOUVILLE LES GONESSES

Monsieur,

**Objet : Compte No:12345\FR\0167**

Je voudrais faire un transfert télégraphique bancaire du compte ci-dessus référencé au profit du compte suivant:

    M. Joe Clements
    Compte No:23456789 code 00-00-01
    Adresse postale : (M. Clements)
    Banque :      (Bank name)
    Adresse postale : (Bank Address)
    Ville:
    Code postal:
    Iban No:

    Date du Transfert: 15\12\2006
    Montant : (Euros \ livres sterling \ autre )

Veuillez avoir l'amabilité de me prévenir dés que l'opération aura été effectuée.

Avec mes remerciements anticipés, veuillez agréer, Monsieur, l'expression de mes sentiments les meilleurs.

Marie Blannin

## Money Transfers

It is vital to know what is happening to money and international transfers. Make sure you have full account details and Iban number for both accounts.

25 The Groves
Winchester
Hampshire
WR7 9PP

22nd March, 2006

Crédit Agricole
Rue du Parc
75000 – PARIS

Dear Sirs,

### Account no: 123 45678

Transfer to French bank account

I have made a transfer from National Westminster Bank, 123 The Mall, Buck House, London EC1 1AA by (telegraphic transfer \ Cheque) for €125,000 to be paid in to the above account.

Please advise me when these funds arrive and the date they will be cleared for use.

Draw bank draft from a French account

I require a bankers draft value £120,000 sterling drawn on the above account and made payable to Joseph Clewins Ltd..

Please advise me when this is available for collection (Please send this to the above address as soon as possible).

Yours faithfully,

John Parkersell

83

Select the paragraph you require and change the addresses to your own and your bank's.

John Parkersell
25 The Groves
Winchester
Hampshire
WR7 9PP

Winchester, le 22 mars 2006

Crédit Agricole
Rue du Parc
75000 – PARIS

Monsieur,

### *Objet : no de compte : 123 45678*

J'ai effectué un transfert de la National Westminster Bank, 123 The Mall, Buck House, London EC1 1AA par (transfert télégraphique \ Chèque ) de 125,000 Euros pour approvisionner le compte cité en référence.

Veuillez avoir l'obligeance de m'aviser lorsque ce virement sera effectué et la date à laquelle je pourrai l'utiliser.

*Transfer to French bank account*

Veuillez avoir l'obligeance de m'adresser un accusé de réception bancaire de la somme de 120,000 livres sterling tirée sur le compte ci-dessus référencé, au profit de Joseph Clewins Ltd.

Veuillez me prévenir dès que cette somme sera utilisable pour encaissement ( veuillez l'expédier à l'adresse ci-dessus dans les meilleurs délais ).

Avec mes remerciements anticipés, veuillez agréer, Monsieur, l'expression de mes sentiments les meilleurs.

*Draw bank draft from a French account*

John Parkersell

# Completing a direct debit mandate

You will be given the opportunity to pay utilities and some local taxes to direct debit. Ask when you set up the account or often the bill will have a mandate attached.

This is a sample of a bill that everybody will get every year – the ubiquitous Taxes Foncieres . The payment slip can be used to enclose with a cheque by post, take in person to your Trésor Public or just complete the direct debit facility on the form.

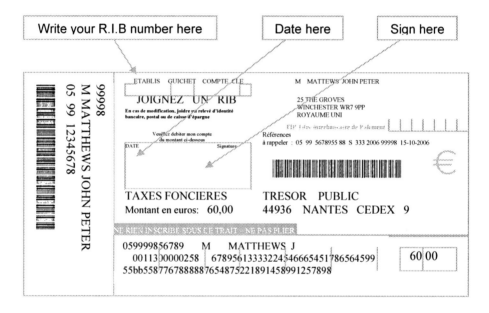

Copies of your R.I.B. (account details) can be found at the back of your cheque book

Although the French banking system is generally very efficient, the bureaucracies of government and utilities frequently are not. Make sure that you check that payments have been made and if not contact the relevant organisation immediately. Late payments attract substantial penalty charges.

## Writing Your French Cheques

Sounds simple, just open the cheque book and write away. Oops! It's not in the same places and what's this "Fait a" ?

Actually, it really is simple once you know where everything goes.

1      Amount in words - in French, of course!

2      Amount in figures

3      Name of person or company to be paid

4      The town where you are when the cheque is written

5      Date

6      Your signature

French figures are puctuacted in reverse of the English style as shown here:

English   159,000.10 euros    French   159.000,10 euros

Follow this simple guide and you will have a perfect cheque without any fuss.

Just a reminder – It is a criminal offence to write a cheque without sufficient funds for immediate payment. At best you will have to pay a penalty and it only takes a few bounced cheques to be banned from holding any account at every bank in France for ten years.

# Chèque d'emploi

For the British, the thought of registering for tax and insurance to pay baby sitters or somebody to cut your grass is alien and few people would give paying for such employment much consideration other than payment by cash in hand. France is very different and paying anybody has to be officially documented and all tax and cotisations paid by the employer.

Fortunately there is a system designed to keep both the employer and employee on the right side of the law and it is known as the Chèque d'emploi system and is very simple to set up.

Call in at the local branch of your French bank or write to them for an application form for a Chèque d'emploi cheque book. Complete the form and return it to your bank and within a couple of weeks (normally) you will get the special cheque book and a supply of the forms that have to be completed every time you write a cheque.

That's the good news – the sting comes when your cheque is presented. The employee recipient gets paid the amount on the cheque but you pay out that amount plus the due tax required plus social insurance charges. Now you know why it is highly expensive to take on employees in France.

Over a million small domestic employers use the Chèque d'emploi system and it keeps the employees up to date with tax, social security and employment payments.

Sadly the benefits of the system have been strangled by bureaucracy and you can only use this payment method for domestic and gardening activities. Before employing anybody for more than a few hours make sure you know where you stand with French employment law. It is possible for somebody to take on a gardener for as little as four hours a week and after a few weeks that person would automatically have a contract of employment with statutory rights to notice period and dismissal procedures. Unlikely to happen, but possible.

2006 has seen the French government move to liberalise employment laws for micro employers and the chèque d'emploi will soon be replaced by chèques universels with slightly lower social charges. Sadly they will still not be available for paying for a wider range of activities and small businesses will not be able to use them.

French bureaucracy takes some time to filter down from the dizzy heights of Paris to the rural expanse of France and the name may change and the payments reduce slightly but you might find yourself using chèque d'emploi paperwork for chèques universels for some time.

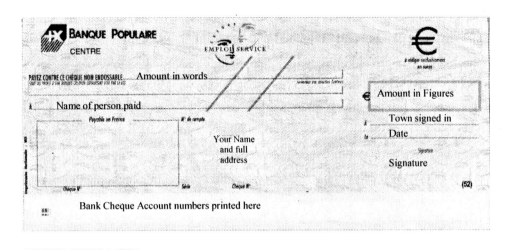

Bank Cheque Account numbers printed here

Filling out the payment chèque d'emploi is exactly the same as a normal cheque. The differences come in the counterfoil that requires more detail than usual.

The volet social is a legal document and requires very careful attention because it is used to calculate the payments for employee social security deductions and tax that are paid by the employer.

# Set up or Change Direct Debits – Standing Order

All of the bank details you require can be found on the R.I.B. pages in your cheque book and the recipient will either give one of these to you or provide the information.

Le Petit Bois
67879 Limoges

3rd December 2006

Crédit Agricole
34, avenue Pierre Semard
95400 Arnouville les Gonesse

Dear Sirs,

**Ref: account No:12345\FR\0167**

Set up

Would you please make arrangements to set up a (direct debit \ standing order) payable to (Mr. \ Mrs. \ Miss) Marion Jones, La forêt, Rue Principale, 535100 - Change account No 3452A6571 at Crédit Mutuel, 7 rue Bretagne 53500 Saint Denis De Gastines,

The first payment of €75 should be made on 10\01\2006 and subsequent payments of €50 each month on the 10th day of the month. (The final payment should be made on 10\11\2006 \ Continue payments until I give written notice).

Change

**Ref: account No:12345\FR\0167**
**(Direct Debit \ Standing order) to Marion Jonas**
Please change the amount of this (Direct Debit \ Standing order) from €25 to €30 with immediate effect (from 10\02\2006).

Cancel

**Ref: account No:12345\FR\0167**
**(Direct Debit \ Standing order) to Marion Jonas**
Please cancel this (Direct Debit \ Standing order) (immediately \ on 10\02\2006)

Yours faithfully,

Marie Blannin

Please be careful with the detailed information required, all variables are in the same order for both English and French versions.

Marie Blannin

Le Petit Bois
67879 Limoges

Limoges, le 3 décembre 2006

Crédit Agricole
34, avenue Pierre Semard
95400 ARNOUVILLE LES GONESSES

Monsieur,

**Réf: compte No:12345\FR\0167**

Veuillez avoir l'obligeance de prendre les dispositions nécessaires au (prélèvement automatique \ virement bancaire) payable à (M. \ Mme. \ Melle) Marion Jones, La forêt, Rue Principale, 535100 – Changé, au compte No 3452A6571 au Crédit Mutuel, 7 rue Bretagne 53500 Saint Denis De Gastines,

Le premier paiement de 75€ sera effectué le 10\01\2006 et les autres, de 50€, chaque mois le 10ème jour du mois. (Le réglement final aura lieu le 10\11\2006 \ En cas d'annulation je vous en informerais par courrier)

**Réf: compte No:12345\FR\0167**
**(Prélèvement automatique \Virement bancaire) _à_ (M. \ Mme. \ Melle)**
**Marion Jonas**

Veuillez avoir l'obligeance de changer le montant de ce (prélèvement automatique \ virement bancaire) de 25€ à 30€ avec effet (immédiat \ à partir du 10\02\2006).

**Réf: compte No:12345\FR\0167**
**(Prélèvement automatique \ Virement bancaire) _à_ (M. \ Mme. \ Melle)**
**Marion Jonas**

Veuillez, s'il vous plaît, arrêter ce (prélèvement automatique \ virement bancaire) (immédiatement \ le 10\02\2006).

Avec mes remerciements anticipés, veuillez agréer, Monsieur, l'expression de mes sentiments distingués.

Marie Blannin

Set up

Change

Cancel

# Request Debit Card and New Cheque Book

Banks are reluctant to post cheque books due to theft – you may have to collect it from the branch.

Grand Mers
St Lucent
66543 Montpellier

23rd October, 2006

Banque Crédit Agricole
Rue St Martin
66550 Montpellier

Dear Sirs

### Account No: 456-8756-01

(I \ We) require a debit card for this account. Would you please supply the form and assist (me \ us) in its completion.

(I \ We) require a new cheque book for this account. (I \ We) will collect it on our next visit to France on 20\11\2006.

Yours Faithfully

John and Mary Parkersell

Select the relevant paragraph for debit card or cheque book.
Change the (singular \ plural) as required and the date of your proposed visit.

John et Mary Parkersell
Grand Mers
 St Lucent
66543 Montpellier

Montpellier, le 23 octobre 2006

> Banque Crédit Agricole
> Rue St Martin
> 66550 Montpellier

Messieurs,

### Numéro de compte 456-8756-01

(Je vous serais reconnaissant \ Nous vous serions reconnaissants) de vouloir bien (m' \ nous ) adresser une carte de retrait bancaire au profit du compte ci-dessus référencé. Veuillez (m' \ nous) informer des démarches nécessaires.

Voudriez-vous avoir l'obligeance de tenir à (ma \ notre) disposition un nouveau chéquier. (Je le retirerai \ Nous le retirerons) à notre prochain voyage en France le 20\11\2006.

Avec (mes \ nos) remerciements anticipés, veuillez agréer, Messieurs, l'expression de (mes \ nos) meilleurs sentiments.

John et Mary Parkersell

Debit Card

Cheque Book

## Repairs or Small Improvements

Just a few of the myriad of small jobs that you may require – many others can be covered by changing the name of the object to be installed or repaired.

Les Petits Bois
53501 - LAVAL

22nd August, 2006

Dear Sirs,

Would you please provide an estimate for the following work:

1. Install a supplied washing machine to existing taps and waste (supplied by you \ supplied by myself).

2. Install a washing machine with new taps and waste (supplied by you \ supplied by myself) in the location shown on the enclosed sketch.

3. Repair a leaking shower unit.

4. Replace a shower unit with a (similar unit to be supplied by yourself \ new unit supplied by (me\us)).

5. Install a new electrical (power point \ light fitting) in the location shown on the enclosed sketch.

6. Replace a damaged electrical (power point \ light fitting).

7. Supply and replace an internal door.

8. Supply and replace an external door.

9. Replace damaged ceramic times with same or similar tiles as per enclosed sketch.

10. Replace ceramic tiled floor as per enclosed sketch.

11. Lay a new ceramic tiled floor as per enclosed sketch.

12. Wall tiling as per enclosed sketch.

(I \ We) await your estimate

Yours faithfully,

Gérard and Marion Broughton

Select the items required carefully – they are numbered in the same order in English and in French.

Gérard et Marion BROUGHTON
Les Petits Bois
53501 - LAVAL

Laval, le 22 août 2006

Monsieur,

Veuillez avoir l'amabilité de (m'adresser \ nous adresser) une estimation (du travail suivant \ des travaux suivants) :

| 1 | Brancher une machine à laver (fournie par vous \ fournie par moi) à la robinetterie et au tuyau d'évacuation existants. |
| 2 | Installer une machine à laver (fournie par vous \ fournie par moi) avec nouvelle robinetterie et tuyau d'évacuation à l'emplacement désigné sur le plan ci-joint. |
| 3 | Réparer la fuite de la douche. |
| 4 | Remplacer le tuyau de douche par un autre (fourni par vous \ fourni par moi ). |
| 5 | Installer une nouvelle ( prise de courant \ lampe ) dans l'emplacement prévu sur le plan ci-joint . |
| 6 | Remplacer ( la prise électrique \ la lampe )  endommagée à l'endroit noté sur le plan ci-joint. |
| 7 | Fournir et poser une porte intérieure en remplacement de celle notée au plan ci-joint. |
| 8 | Fournir et poser une porte extérieure en remplacement de celle notée au plan ci-joint. |
| 9 | Remplacer la partie de céramique endommagée par des carreaux semblables tel que prévu au plan ci-joint. |
| 10 | Remplacer la partie de carrelage prévue au plan ci-joint. |
| 11 | Poser un nouveau carrelage comme prévu au plan ci-joint. |
| 12 | Poser une faïence sur la partie de mur prévue au plan ci-joint. |

Avec (mes \ nos) remerciements anticipés ainsi que (mes \ nos) meilleurs sentiments.


Gérard et Marion Broughton

# Obtain an Estimate from an Artisan

Make sure you select an appropriate artisan to do the work you require. Few will undertake work other than their specialised field.

Les Petits-Bois
53872 - LAVAL

12th April, 2006

Les Artisans
Zone Artisanale
35642 Mayenne.

Dear Sirs,

### Le Petit Bois, St Pierre, 53872 Laval

Would you please provide an estimate for the following work:

Plaster walls and ceilings as per enclosed (sketch \ plan).

(Replace \ Install) kitchen units (supplied \ to be supplied by yourself)

(Replace \ Install) (bathroom \ shower room) (supplied \ to be supplied by yourself)

I would ask that you advise me(us) of a date and time that is convenient to yourself (I \ We) will be in France between 10\05\2004 and 18\05\2004.

Yours faithfully,

Gerald and Marion Clements

Select the paragraph you require and edit it to your needs by deleting the appropriate phrases. They are in the same order as the English version

Gerald et Marion Clements
Les Petits-Bois
53872 - LAVAL

Laval, le 12 avril 2006

Les Artisans
Zone Artisanale
35642 Mayenne.

Monsieur,

**<u>Le Petit Bois, St Pierre, 53872 Laval</u>**

Voudriez-vous avoir l'amabilité de prévoir un devis pour les travaux suivants:

Enduire en plâtre les murs et plafonds comme prévu au plan ci-joint.

(Remplacer \ Installer) les éléments de cuisine (approvisionnés sur place \ fournis par vous ).

(Remplacer \ Installer) ( la salle de bains \ la douche ) (approvisionnée sur place \ fournie par vous ).

(Nous vous demanderons \ Je vous demanderais) de me prévenir de la date et de l'heure qui vous conviendraient sachant que nous serons en France du 10\05\2004 au 18\05\2004.

Avec mes remerciements et mes meilleurs sentiments.

Gerald et Marion Clements

## Accept Estimate and get Start Date

You may well be asked to sign the estimate (devis) when you send this letter. This makes the contract between yourself and the artisan a legally binding contract. Make sure you insert start and complertion dates for the work.

25 The Groves
Winchester
Hampshire
WR7 9PP
2<sup>nd</sup> September, 2006

M. Jean Picard
Maçon
Rue de Picot
66579 Montpellier

Dear Sirs,

### Grand Mers, St Lucent, 66543 Montpellier

(I \ We) accept your Estimate No: 675677  and agree the charges for work to be carried out at the above property.

Please contact (me \ us) as soon as possible with a start date and estimate of the time required for completion of the work.

(I \ We) agree that payment will be 30% on start of work and payments of 70% on completion).

Yours Faithfully,

John and Mary Parkersell

Accept the paragraph required and remember to change the (singular \ plural as required)

John et Mary Parkersell
25 The Groves
Winchester
Hampshire
WR7 9PP

Winchester, le 2 septembre 2006

M. Jean Picard
Maçon
Rue de Picot
66579 Montpellier

**<u>Grand Mers, St Lucent, 66543 Montpellier</u>**

Monsieur,

 (J'accepte \ Nous acceptons votre *<u>devis N° 675677</u>* et  (vous charge \ vous chargeons) de mener à bien ce travail sur (ma \ notre) propriété.

Veuillez (me \ nous) informer, dans les meilleurs délais, de la date à laquelle vous comptez mettre en chantier et de la durée estimée de ces travaux.

(J'accepte \ Nous acceptons) le réglement de ces travaux comme prévu à votre devis à savoir: 30% au démarrage du chantier -   acomptes de 70% au fur et à mesure de l'avancement des travaux  sur présentation  de l'estimation  de leur coût et solde à l'achèvement.

Veuillez recevoir, Monsieur, l'assurance de (mes \ nos) meilleurs sentiments.


John Parkersell     Mary Parkersell

# Find Local Artisans

What better source of local tradesmen and craftsmen than the mairie who know about everybody in business in their area.

---

Le Petit Bois
53000
CHANGE

10<sup>th</sup> October 2006

The Mayor of Changé
53000 – CHANGE

Dear Sirs,

### Le Petit Bois 53000 Changé

(I \ We) will be renovating the above property and would like to use local artisans.

Would you be kind enough to let me have a list of artisans within your administrative area for the following trades:

> Roofer
> General builder
> Bricklayer (Stonemason)
> Electrician
> Plumber
> JCB earth works (foundations)
> Architect
> Kitchen fitter

(I \ We) await your reply,

Yours faithfully,

Jason and Joy Harmers

---

Just delete the trades you don't need and change the (singular \ plural) as required.

Jason et Joy Harmers
Le Petit Bois
53000
CHANGÉ

Changé, le 10 octobre 2006

Monsieur le Maire de Changé
53000 - CHANGÉ

Objet : ma propriété  Le Petit Bois Cne de Changé
Demande de liste d'artisans

Monsieur,

(J'ai \ Nous avons)  l'intention de rénover la propriété citée en référence avec l'aide des artisans de la Commune ou de la Région.

Voudriez-vous avoir l'obligeance de (m'\ nous) adresser une liste des artisans de votre Commune et des alentours exerçant les professions suivantes:
> Charpentier-couvreur
> Entreprise générale de construction
> Maçon
> Electricien
> Plombier
> Entreprise de travaux public ou privé pour fouilles et étalement
> Architecte
> Installateur de cuisine

(Je vous remercie \ Nous vous remercions)  de votre réponse.

Veuillez agréer, Monsieur, l'expression de (mes \ nos) meilleurs sentiments.

Jason et Joy Harmers

## SIRET and Insurance

Before commissioning any work, check out the contractor. Only registered artisans offer a ten year guarantee on work and enable you to claim their invoice against future capital gains tax.

Le Petit Bois
53567 Laval

2nd May 2006

Mr. Philippe JOLLIET
Maçon
LAVAL
53300 – LAVAL

Dear Sirs,

Thank you for your estimate for work to be carried out at (my \ our) property.

Before (I \ we) make a decision about the work (I \ we) would ask for details of your SIRET registration number and what insurance cover you have. Details of any guarantee given on your work would be appreciated.

You mentioned that you had undertaken similar work in the area and ((I \ we) would like two names of previous clients as references for your work.

When we have this information (I \ we) will be in a position to make a decision on whether to proceed.

Yours faithfully

John and Mary Matthews.

Change the bracketed singular and plural as required.

John et Mary Matthews
Le Petit Bois
53567 Laval

Laval, le 2 mai 2006

Monsieur Philippe JOLLIET
Maçon
LAVAL
53300 – LAVAL

Monsieur,

(Je vous remercie\ Nous vous remercions) pour votre devis relatif aux travaux envisagés sur (ma \ notre) propriété.

Cependant, avant de prendre une décision concernant ce travail (je vous serais obligée \ nous vous serions obligés) de (me \ nous) faire connaître le numéro de votre Siret et le nom de la Compagnie d'assurance qui couvre votre entreprise en garantie décénale.

D'autre part veuillez (me \ nous) faire savoir quels chantiers identiques vous avez entrepris dans la région et (me \ nous) communiquer les coordonnées de deux de vos précédents clients.

Dés réception de ces informations (je prendrai \ nous prendrons) une décision.

Recevez (mes \ nos) remerciements ainsi que (mes \ nos) sentiments les meilleurs.

John et Mary Matthews

## Central Heating Quotation

A simple sketch or plan can make the understanding of what is required much easier for the artisan preparing the quotation

---

Les Petits-Bois
53872 - LAVAL

12 September, 2006

M. PICARD Jean
Sarl Picard Plombier
Rue de la Forêt
53563 Laval

Dear Mr. Picard,

**<u>Le Petit Bois, 53756 Laval</u>**

The above property requires a new central heating installation (using the existing boiler \ with a new boiler) and  (I \ we) would appreciate a meeting with yourself to obtain an estimate for the work.

Enclosed is a (sketch \ plan) showing the work required.

Materials should be of a quality to ensure acceptance by the water company.

Please advise (me \ us) of a date and time that is suitable for yourself.  (I \ We} will be available between 10\10\2006 and 15\10\2006 for a meeting.

Yours faithfully,

John and Marion Jamison

---

Change the dates to suit your arrangements and select the choices from the bracketed selection. They are in the same order as the English letter.

John et Marion Jamison
Les Petits-Bois
53872 - LAVAL

Laval, le 12 septembre 2006

> M. Jean Picard
> Sarl Picard Plombier
> Rue de la Forêt
> 53563 Laval

Monsieur,

### Le Petit Bois, 53756 Laval

La propriété ci-dessus référencée a besoin d'une nouvelle installation de chauffage central (tout en conservant la chaudière existante qui est en excellent état \ avec une chaudière neuve ) et (j'apprécierai \ nous apprécierions )une rencontre avec vous pour déterminer les détails de ce travail et avoir une estimation de son coût.

Sous ce pli veuillez bien trouver le (croquis \ plan) de ce projet.

Veuillez vous assurer que le matériel que vous utiliserez est bien conforme aux normes recommandées par la Compagnie des Eaux.

Veuillez bien (me \ nous) faire savoir à quelle date et à quelle heure nous pourrons nous rencontrer sachant que (je serai \ nous serons) en France du 10\10\2006 au 15\10\2006.

Recevez (mes \ nos) remerciements anticipés ainsi que (mes \ nos) sentiments les meilleurs.


John et Marion Jamison

# Electrical rewire quotation

25 The Groves
Winchester
Hampshire
WR7 9PP

2$^{nd}$ September, 2006

M. Jean Picard
Electricien
Rue de Picot
66579 Montpellier

Dear Sir,

## **Grand Mers, St Lucent, 66543 Montpellier**

The above property requires major electrical rewiring work and (I \ we) would appreciate a meeting with yourself to obtain an estimate for the work.

Enclosed is a (sketch \ plan) showing the work required.

Materials should be of a quality to ensure acceptance by EDF.

Please advise (me \ us) of a date and time that is suitable for yourself .(I \ We} will be available in France between  29\09\2006 and 07\11\2006 for a meeting.

Yours faithfully,

John Parkersell

Select the bracketed choices and remember to change the dates.

John Parkersell
25 The Groves
Winchester
Hampshire
WR7 9PP

Winchester, le 2 septembre 2006

M. Jean Picard
Electricien
Rue de Picot
66579 Montpellier

Monsieur,

### **Grand Mers, St Lucent, 66543 Montpellier**

La propriété mentionnée ci-dessus a besoin d'une révision de son installation électrique et j'aimerais vous rencontrer sur place pour en définir les modalités et que vous puissiez m'en faire une estimation.

Sous ce pli je joins un (croquis \ un plan) des travaux prévus.

Pourriez vous vous assurez que le matériel que vous aurez l'intention d'utiliser sera de qualité conforme aux exigences de sécurité recommandées par EDF.

Pourriez –vous me faire savoir à quelle date et à quelle heure vous serez disponible pour un rendez-vous, sachant que (je serai \ nous serons) en France du 29\09\2006 au 7\11\2006.

Recevez (mes \ nos) remerciements anticipés ainsi que (mes \ nos) meilleurs sentiments.

John Parkersell

# Roof quotation

Select the work required and enclose a sketch or plan if you are having any changes from the original roof.

25 The Groves
Winchester
Hampshire
WR7 9PP
2<sup>nd</sup> September, 2006

M. Jean Picard
Charpentier-couvreur
Rue de Picot
66579 Montpellier

Dear Sir,

### Grand Mers, St Lucent, 66543 Montpellier

The above property requires (major roof repairs \ complete re-roofing) and (I \ we) would appreciate a meeting with yourself to obtain an estimate for the work.

Enclosed is a (sketch \ plan) showing the work involved and window positions.

Materials should be (slate \ tiles) in keeping with other properties nearby.

Please advise (me \ us) of a date and time that is suitable for yourself .(I \ We} will be available in France between 12\11\2006 et le 19\11\2006 for a meeting.

Yours faithfully,

Gerald  and Marion Clements

Take care with the changes and dates – they are in the same order as the English letter.

---

Gerald et Marion Clements
25 The Groves
Winchester
Hampshire
WR7 9PP

Winchester, le 2 septembre 2006

M. Jean Picard
Charpentier-couvreur
Rue de Picot
66579 Montpellier

Monsieur,

## Grand Mers, St Lucent, 66543 Montpellier

La majeure partie de la couverture de cette propriété doit être (révisée \ refaite) et j'aimerais avoir une réunion avec vous sur place pour en définir les modalités et que vous puissiez m'en faire une estimation.

Ci-joint (un croquis \ un plan) des travaux à envisager.

Pourriez-vous vous assurez que les (ardoises \ tuiles) que vous utiliserez respecteront le style des propriétés du voisinage.

(Sachant que (je serai \ nous serons) en France entre le 12\11\2006 et le 19\11\2006 pourriez vous nous indiquer le jour et l'heure où nous pourrions vous rencontrer.

Recevez (mes \ nos) remerciements anticipés ainsi que (mes \ nos) sentiments les meilleurs.


Gerald et Marion Clements

---

# Window quotation

Check whether you need planning consent for any changes, especially if you are altering sizes.

---

25 The Groves
Winchester
Hampshire
WR7 9PP

$2^{nd}$ September, 2006

M. Jean Picard
Charpentier-couvreur
Rue de Picot
66579 Montpellier

Dear Sir,

**<u>Grand Mers, St Lucent, 66543 Montpellier</u>**

The above property requires (a new window \ new windows \ door \ doors ) installed in the existing wall as shown on the enclosed (sketch \ plan) and (I \ we) would appreciate a meeting with yourself to obtain an estimate for the work.

Materials should be of a quality to comply with any relevant building regulations.

Please advise (me \ us) of a date and time that is suitable for yourself. (I \ We} will be available in France between 12\11\2006 and 19\11\2006 for a meeting.

Yours faithfully,

Gerald  and Marion Clements

---

Careful with the choice of windows(s) \ door(s) and the and (singular \ plural choices.

---

Gerald et Marion Clements
25 The Groves
Winchester
Hampshire
WR7 9PP

Winchester, le 2 septembre 2006

M. Jean Picard
Charpentier-couvreur
Rue de Picot
66579 Montpellier

Monsieur,

### Grand Mers, St Lucent, 66543 Montpellier

Cette propriété a besoin (qu'une nouvelle fenêtre \ que de nouvelles fenêtres \ porte soit installée \ portes soient installées) dans (la façade notée \ les façades notées) au ( croquis \ plan ) ci-joint et j'aimerais avoir une réunion avec vous sur place pour en définir les modalités et que vous puissiez m'en faire une estimation.

Vous vous assurerez que le matériel que vous utiliserez est de bonne qualité et conforme avec la réglementation en matière de construction normale.

Sachant que (je serai \ nous serons) en France entre le 12\11\2006 et le 19\11\2006 pourriez-vous (m' \ nous) informer du jour et de l'heure où vous serez disponible pour ( me \ nous) rencontrer sur place.

Recevez (mes \ nos) remerciements anticipés ainsi que (mes \ nos) meilleurs sentiments.

Gerald et Marion Clements

## What guarantee is offered ?

Many artisans in France are required to offer substantial guarantees for their work, especially those connected with the building trade. A very good reason for checking that your artisan is working legitimately and not "On the Black".

25 The Groves
Winchester
Hampshire
WR7 9PP

22nd March, 2006

Fouilleul (SARL)
zone artisanale Vallées
53300 Ambrierres les Vallées
France

Dear Sir,

**<u>Estimate No: 123456</u>**

Before making a decision on placing the contract for this work I would like to know what guarantee is offered on the materials and work to be undertaken.

Yours faithfully,

Gérard and Marion Broughton

Just one selection singular or plural in the last line.

Gérard et Marion Broughton
25 The Groves
Winchester
Hampshire
WR7 9PP

Winchester, le 22 mars 2006

Fouilleul (SARL)
Zone artisanale Vallées
53300 Ambrierres les Vallées
France

Monsieur,

### *Votre Devis No 12530*

Avant de prendre une décision d'engagement pour ce travail je voudrais savoir quelle garantie vous accordez sur le matériel et le travail à entreprendre.

Dans l'attente de votre réponse et avec mes remerciements anticipés, recevez, Monsieur, (mes \ nos) meilleures salutations.

Gérard et Marion Broughton

# Confirm fees and give estimate

Very similar wording in English but a huge difference in French.

Grand Mers
St Lucent
66543 Montpellier


23rd October, 2006

Jacques Perrier,
Maçon,
53509 St Hilare.


Dear Mr Perrier

**Grand Mers, St Lucent, 66543 Montpellier**

*Professional:* Bank – Lawyer - Surveyor

Thank you for meeting (me \ us) at the above property. Would you please confirm your fees and work to be undertaken as discussed during our meeting on 22\ 10\2004.


*Artisan builder, plumber, electrician etc*

Thank you for meeting (me \ us) at the above property. Would you please confirm your price and list work to be undertaken in a detailed estimate, as discussed during our meeting on 22\10\2004.


Yours faithfully,



John and Mary Parkersell

Select the appropriate paragraph for the type of business you are dealing with.

John et Mary Parkersell
Grand Mers
St Lucent
66543 Montpellier

Montpellier, le 23 octobre 2006

Jacques Perrier,
Maçon,
53509 St Hilare.

Cher Monsieur Perrier,

### *Ref: Propriété :* **Grand Mers, St Lucent, 66543 Montpellier**

(Je vous remercie \ Nous vous remercions) d'avoir bien voulu (me \ nous) rencontrer à la propriété citée en référence. Veuillez avoir l'obligeance de (me \ nous) confirmer le montant de vos émoluments et le détail des travaux à entreprendre dans le cadre de la discussion que (j'ai eue \ que nous avons eue) avec vous lors de ce rendez-vous du 22\10\2004.

Recevez, cher Monsieur, avec (mes \ nos) remerciements, l'expression de (mes \ nos) sentiments les meilleurs.

*Professional*

(Je vous remercie \ Nous vous remercions) d'avoir bien voulu venir me rencontrer en la propriété citée en référence. Voudriez-vous avoir l'obligeance de m'adresser un devis descriptif et estimatif des travaux à entreprendre dans le cadre de la discussion que nous avons eue lors de notre rendez-vous du 22\10\2004.

(Je vous remercie \ Nous vous remercions) bien vivement à l'avance et vous adresse mes meilleurs sentiments.

*Artisan*

John et Mary Parkersell

## Builders Merchants order

Don't know the translation for the item – use the catalogues or the word list to be found at: http:\\normandy.angloinfo.com\information\3\buildingjargon.asp

Le Petit Bois
67879 Limoges

3rd December 2006

Point P
67877 Limoges

Dear Sirs,

**1** Please supply the following for collection on 10\12\2006:

**2** Please supply the following for delivery on 10\12\2006 to the above address.

| Quantity | Item | Size | Price |
|----------|------|------|-------|
|          |      |      |       |

Payment will be (made on delivery \ with the order) by (cheque \ credit card \ debit card \ by account).

Please confirm the date of delivery and total price.

Yours faithfully.

Joseph Blannin

Select the paragraph for collection or delivery as required and delete unwanted payment details

Joseph Blannin
Le Petit Bois
67879 Limoges

Limoges, le 3 décembre 2006

$\qquad$ Point P
67877 Limoges

Messieurs,

Je vous serais reconnaissant de bien vouloir préparer les matériaux suivants que je viendrai chercher le 10\12\2006.
A savoir :

1

Je vous serais reconnaissant de bien vouloir me fournir les matériaux suivants et de me les livrer à l'adresse ci-dessus le 10\12\2006.
A savoir :

2

**QUANTITÉ**     **ARTICLE**     **DIMENSIONS**     **PRIX**

Le réglement se fera à la (livraison ou \ commande) par (chèque\ carte de crédit \ carte à débit immédiat \ en espèces).

Veuillez me confirmer la date de cette livraison et le prix.

Sentiments distingués.

Joseph Blannin

# Hire JCB Digger - With \ Without Driver

It is economic to hire heavy plant for short periods and qualified drivers are often available.

Le Petit Bois
53567 Laval

2 May, 2006

Kiloutou
Locatieon de Materiel
35132 Rennes - Vezin

Dear Sirs,

### Le Petit Bois, 53567 Laval

JCB With Driver

(I \ We) require a JCB digger with a (600 mm \ 450 mm \ 300 mm) bucket together with a trained driver for earthwork as per the enclosed sketch.

The machine should be delivered to the above address on 25\05\2006 at 15.00 hours and collected on completion of the work.

JCB Without Driver

(I \ We) require a JCB digger for (3) days ,with a (600 mm \ 450 mm \ 300 mm) bucket without a driver.

The machine should be delivered to the above address on 22\05\2006 at 09.00 hours and collected on completion of the work.

Please confirm availability and price for this.

Yours faithfully,

Mary Matthews

117

Select the paragraph to fit your needs and change the dates, hire period and (singular \ plural) as required.

Mary Matthews
Le Petit Bois
53567 Laval

Laval, le 2 mai 2006

Kiloutou
Location de Matériel
35132 Rennes - Vezin

Messieurs,

**Le Petit Bois, 53567 Laval**

(Je souhaiterais \ Nous souhaiterions) louer un excavateur JCB avec ses godets de (600 mm \ 450 mm \ 300 mm) avec chauffeur qualifié pour terrassement et fouilles pour fondations.

 La machine devra être livrée à l'adresse ci-dessus le 25\05\2006 à 15.00 heures et reprise à l'achèvement des travaux.

(Je vous remercie \ Nous vous remercions) de me confirmer cette location et de m'en faire connaître le prix.

(Je souhaiterais \ Nous souhaiterions) louer pour (3) jours, un excavateur JCB avec ses godets de (600 mm \ 450 mm \ 300 mm) sans chauffeur.

La machine devra être livrée à l'adresse ci-dessus le 25\05\2006 à 15.00 heures et reprise à l'achèvement des travaux.

Voudriez-vous me confirmer si cette location est possible et m'en donner le prix.

Veuillez agréer, Monsieur, l'expression de (mes \ nos) meilleurs sentiments.

Mary Matthews

# Hire tools from hire companies

Not sure of the french name for a tool?   Try this web page:
http:\\normandy.angloinfo.com\information\3\buildingjargon.asp

---

Le Petit Bois
53567 Laval

2<sup>nd</sup> May, 2006

Kiloutou
Location de Matériel
35132 Rennes - Vezin

Messieurs,

### Le Petit Bois, 53567 Laval

I wish to hire a dehumidifier from 25\05\2006 to 30\05\2006 for use at the above address.

A copy of my passport and (an electricity \ a gas \ a water) bill will be provided for identification.

|1| Please advise me of the total cost including V.A.T. and delivery.

|2| Please advise me of the total cost including V.A.T. I will collect the dehumidifier from your premises.

Yours faithfully,

Mary Matthews.

Choose the paragraph for delivery or collection, change the dates and select the means of identification.

Mary Matthews
Le Petit Bois
53567 Laval

Laval, le 2 mai 2006

Kiloutou
Location de Matériel
35132 Rennes - Vezin

Messieurs,

**Le Petit Bois, 53567 Laval**

Je désire louer un déshumidificateur du 25\05\2006 au 30\05\2006 pour utilisation à l'adresse ci-dessus.

Je vous adresse une copie de mon passeport et une facture (d'EDF \ GDF \ Eau) prouvant mon identité.

Voudriez-vous me chiffrer le coût de cette location TVA et livraison incluses.  1

Veuillez me chiffrer le coût de cette location TVA incluse; je viendrai prendre livraison de ce matériel loué dans vos locaux.  2

Avec mes remerciements et mes meilleurs sentiments.

Mary Matthews

# Carte de Séjour

Make sure you have all of the required documents as required. The requirement for a Carte de Séjour is being abolished but French officialdom takes time to realise the law has changed.

Le Petit Bois
53567 Laval

2nd May 2006

Monsieur le Maire
Hotel de Ville
Place du 11 Novembre
53300 - LAVAL

Dear Mr Mayor,

I enclose an application form and supporting documents for a Carte de Séjour.

Enclosed are 2 photcopies of the following:

**Identity**
Passport
Three black & white passport photos     *(photo booths pictures are ok)*
Birth certificate
Marriage Certificate    *(if applicable)*
Birth certificates of children    *(if applicable)*
EDF or similar bill    *(in your name)*
Acte de Vente
 or rental agreement

**Income**  (choose appropriate categories)
Contract of employment    *(if employed for **Activ** category)*
Proof of pension income    *(if retired for **Non-Activ** category)*
Proof of enrolment at college and proof of income    *(for **Etudiant** category)*
when main applicant is a student.

Two self addressed envelopes

Issue of a temporary permit is requested.

Yours faithfully,

John  and Mary Matthews

All of the documents listed are required.

Choose one of the income options and delete the others.

---

John et Mary Matthews
Le Petit Bois
53567 Laval

Laval, le 2 mai 2006

Monsieur le Maire
Hôtel de Ville
Place du 11 Novembre
53300 - LAVAL

Monsieur le Maire ,

Je vous adresse ci-joint un formulaire et les différents documents afférents à ma demande de carte de séjour.

Je joins également 2 photocopies des pièces ci-après détaillées:

**Identité**

Passeport
3 photos en noir et blanc pour passeport
Certificat de naissance
Certificat de mariage
Quittance EDF
Acte de vente
ou Bail de location

**Revenus**
Ressources
Contrat de travail
Quittance de pension ou retraite
Preuve d'inscription au collège et preuve de revenus

2 enveloppes à mon adresse.

Veuillez avoir l'obligeance de m'en adresser récépissé.

Avec mes remerciements anticipés pour la bonne suite que vous voudrez bien apporter à ma demande, veuillez agréer, Monsieur le Maire, l'expression de mes meilleurs sentiments.

John et Mary Matthews

---

## Do I need a Carte de Séjour

The law may have changed but it might still be easier to apply for the Carte de Séjour if the mairie insists. Asking if it is still required might bring back a favourable answer.

Les Petits Bois
53501 - LAVAL

22nd August, 2006

Monsieur le Maire
Hotel de Ville
Place de 11 Novembre
53300 - LAVAL

Dear Mr Mayor,

I wish to apply for a Carte de Séjour but I am not sure if this is required since the passing of the European Union Article 14 of law number 2003-1119 of 26 November 2003.

Would you be kind enough to confirm if this is now a condition of residence in France for citizens of the United Kingdom.

Should this still be required please let me have the appropriate application forms for (myself \ myself and wife \ partner \ and children ages, 3, 6 and 11 years).

Yours faithfully,

Gérard Broughton

Take care with the options for your family – they are in the same order in English and French.

---

Gérard BROUGHTON
Les Petits Bois
53501 - LAVAL


Laval, le 22 août 2006

> Monsieur le Maire
> Hôtel de Ville
> Place du 11 Novembre
> 53300 - LAVAL


Monsieur le Maire,

Je désirerais obtenir une carte de séjour mais j'ignore si cela est toujours nécessaire depuis l'article 14 de l'Union Européenne- Article non défini.

Pourriez-vous me faire savoir si cette carte est toujours obligatoire pour les citoyens anglais voulant résider en France?

Si cette formalité est nécessaire, veuillez avoir l'obligeance de m'adresser le formulaire approprié pour (moi \ ma femme \ partenaire \ et mes enfants âgés de 3, 6 et 11 ans).

Je vous en remercie bien vivement à l'avance.

Veuillez agréer, Monsieur le Maire, l'expression de mes sentiments les meilleurs.



Gérard Broughton

---

# Get Information on the Town or Area

An incredible amount of information can be found at La Mairie of your village or town.

Les Petits-Bois
53872 - LAVAL

12th April, 2006

Mairie de Laval
Place du 11 Novembre
53013 LAVAL Cedex

Dear Mr. Mayor,

### Le Petit Bois, 53756 Laval

(I \ We) have recently (moved in to \ purchased) the above property and would like to have copies of any brochures giving details of the (town \ village), activities and facilities to be found in the area

(I \ We) are considering purchasing a property in (*Name of Village*) and would like to have copies of any brochures giving details of the (town \ village), activities and facilities to be found in the area

Yours faithfully,

John Peterson

Purchased

Considering

Take care with the many selection in this letter – all options are in the same order as the English version.

John Peterson
Les Petits-Bois
53872 - LAVAL

Laval, le 12 avril 2006

Mairie de Laval
Place du 11 Novembre
53013 LAVAL Cedex

Monsieur le Maire,

**Le Petit Bois, 53756 Laval**

(J'habite \ Nous habitons ) (Depuis peu  (j'ai \  nous avons) acheté la propriété mentionnée ci-dessus et (je souhaiterais \ nous souhaiterions ) recevoir des brochures au sujet de votre (ville \ village) et de la région alentour : les activités , loisirs, commerces etc..

(J'ai \ Nous avons) l'intention d'acheter une propriété dans votre (ville \ village) et (j'aimerais \ nous aimerions) recevoir des brochures au sujet des activités, loisirs,  commerces etc.. de votre (ville \ village ) et de la région alentour.

(Je vous remercie \Nous vous remercions) de votre amabilité et (vous prie \ vous prions) d'agréer, Monsieur le Maire, l'expression de (mes \  nos) sentiments les meilleurs.

John Peterson.

Purchased

Considering

# List of Officially Approved Translators

Many official applications can only accept English documents like marriage certificates and driving licences if the are accompanied by approved translators.

Les Petits-Bois
53872 - LAVAL

12<sup>th</sup> April, 2006

Mairie de Laval
Place du 11 Novembre
53013 LAVAL Cedex

Dear Mr Mayor

(I \ We) need to have documents translated from English to French by a translator approved to certify translation of official documents.

Could you please supply is list of translators within the region who are qualified and approved to carry out this work.

Yours faithfully,

Joan and Phillip Peterson

Just the singular\ plural options to select

Joan et Phillip Peterson
Les Petits-Bois
53872 - LAVAL

Laval, le 12 avril 2006

Mairie de Laval
Place du 11 Novembre
53013 LAVAL Cedex

Monsieur le Maire,

(J'ai \ Nous avons) besoin de faire traduire des documents anglais en français par un traducteur agréé garantissant l'authenticité des documents.

Voudriez-vous avoir l'obligeance de (m'adresser \ nous adresser) une liste des traducteurs agréés existant dans votre région  pouvant réaliser ce travail.

Avec (mes \ nos) remerciements anticipés, veuillez agréer, Monsieur le Maire, l'expression de (mes \ nos) meilleurs sentiments.

Joan et Phillip Peterson

# Names of Surveyors for Fosse Septique Étude

Forget the stories of "just put it where you want" – new laws require a report by an approved surveyor before you can even apply to install a fosse septique. Only the mairie can provide the list you require.

Les Petits-Bois
53872 - LAVAL

12th April, 2006

Mairie de Laval
Place du 11 Novembre
53013 LAVAL Cedex

Dear Mr. Mayor

**Les Petits-Bois  53872 - LAVAL**

(I \ We) need to have a fosse septique installed for the above.

Could you please supply a list of approved surveyors to carry out the required survey together with the fees that would normally be charged for this work.

Yours faithfully,

Phillip Peterson

Make the (singular \ plural choices) as required.

Phillip Peterson
Les Petits-Bois
53872 - LAVAL

Laval, le 12 avril 2006

> Mairie de Laval
> Place du 11 Novembre
> 53013 LAVAL Cedex

Monsieur le Maire,

### Les Petits-Bois  53872 - LAVAL

(J'ai \ Nous avons) besoin de faire installer une fosse septique sur cette propriété.

Voudriez-vous avoir l'obligeance de (m'adresser \ nous adresser) une liste d'Ingénieurs agréés du Service Sanitaire pouvant étudier ce projet ainsi qu'un aperçu de la rémunération normalement prévue dans ce cas.

(Je vous en remercie \ Nous vous en remercions)  bien vivement à l'avance.

(Je vous prie \ Nous vous  prions) d'agréer, Monsieur le Maire, l'expression de (mes \ nos) sentiments les meilleurs.

Phillip Peterson.

# French language courses

The mairie is the source of information on many subjects and many organise courses for non French speakers.

Les Petits-Bois
53872 - LAVAL

12<sup>th</sup> April, 2006

Mairie de Laval
Place du 11 Novembre
53013 LAVAL Cedex

Dear Mr Mayor,

(I \ We) have recently moved (in to \ purchased) the above property and would like to improve (my \ our) knowledge of the French language to assist (my \ our) integration in the community.

Would you be kind enough to inform (me \ us) of any French language courses that may be suitable and are held in the area.

Yours faithfully,

John Peterson

Select the desired (singular \ plural) choices and the (town \ village) option.

John Peterson
Les Petits-Bois
53872 - LAVAL

Laval, le 12 avril 2006

> Mairie de Laval
> Place du 11 Novembre
> 53013 LAVAL Cedex

Monsieur le Maire,

(J'habite \ Nous habitons) (Depuis peu j'ai acheté \ Depuis peu nous avons acheté) la propriété citée en référence et (j'aimerais \ nous aimerions) améliorer (ma \ notre) connaissance de la langue Française pour (me \ nous) permettre une meilleure intégration au coeur de la communauté de votre (ville \ village).

Voudriez-vous avoir l'amabilité de (m'informer \ nous informer) des cours de Langue Française enseignés dans votre (ville \ village) ou dans un rayon proche?

(Je vous en remercie \ Nous vous en remercions) bien vivement à l'avance.

(Je vous prie \ Nous vous prions) d'agréer, Monsieur le Maire, l'expression de (mes \ nos ) sentiments les meilleurs.

John Peterson

## Querying tax d'habitation

Sometimes you will receive a demand for this tax before the property is in a condition to be lived in. Send this letter to the address on the demand and you should become exempt until work is finished.

25 The Groves
Winchester
Hampshire
WR7 9PP

22nd March, 2006

Hotel de Ville
Place du 11 Novembre
53300 - LAVAL

Dear Sirs,

**Taxe d'habitation ref: 53\0123478\2006**

I have received the enclosed demand for payment of tax d'habitation and must ask that you note that the property is not inhabited or fit for habitation at this time.

I will notify you when the property has been restored to a state where Tax d'habitation is applicable.

Yours faithfully,

Gérard and Marion Broughton

Just make sure the reference number and the address you send the letter to
are identical to that on the actual demand.

Gérard et Marion Broughton
25 The Groves
Winchester
Hampshire
WR7 9PP

Winchester, le 22 mars 2006

Hôtel de Ville
Place du 11 Novembre
53300 - LAVAL

**Taxe d'habitation ref: 53\0123478\2006**

Monsieur ,

(J'ai reçu \ Nous ai reçu) la demande de réglement ci-inclus de la taxe
d'habitation et je voudrais vous informer que la propriété n'est pas encore
habitée et n'est pas habitable dans son état actuel .

(Je vous préviendrai \ Nous vous préviendrions) lorsque la propriété sera
restaurée et habitable.

(Je vous remercie \ Nous vous remercions) à l'avance de bien vouloir prendre
note de cet état et éventuellement, de diligenter une enquête sur place.

(Je vous prie \ Nous vous prions) d'agréer, Monsieur, l'expression de (mes \ nos)
sentiments distingués.

Gérard et Marion Broughton.

## Roof Grants

When you have been living and paying taxes in France for more than 2 years you may be eligible for roofing grants. Some regions make grants, others do not. Asking at the mairie is the only sure way to find out.

---

Les Petits Bois
53501 - LAVAL

22nd August, 2006

Monsieur le Maire
La Mairie
53000 - LAVAL

Dear Mr. Mayor,

### Les Petits Bois, 53501 - LAVAL

The above property requires major roof work and (I \ we) would appreciate your opinion as to the availability of grants to assist with this work.

The property is being renovated for (my own use \ our own use \ to be rented to a resident of this area).

Should grants we available (I \ we) would appreciate a list of the criteria required and conditions applicable to the application.

Yours faithfully

Gérard and Marion Broughton

---

Gérard et Marion BROUGHTON
Les Petits Bois
53501 - LAVAL

Laval, le 22 août 2006

Monsieur le Maire
La Mairie
53000 - LAVAL

Monsieur,

## Les Petits Bois, 53501 - LAVAL

Cette propriété a besoin d'un important travail de révision de couverture et nous voudrions connaître votre opinion sur la possibilité d'une subvention pour aider au financement de ce travail.

Cette propriété a été rénovée pour (mon usage personnel \ notre usage personnel \ pour location à des résidents du secteur ).

Si cette subvention peut être octroyée voudriez-vous avoir l'amabilité d'établir une liste de ces travaux avec les critères applicables en pareille matière?

Recevez (mes \ nos) remerciements anticipés ainsi que l'expression de (mes \ nos) meilleurs sentiments.

Gérard et Marion Broughton

## Mini Station d'épuration

Where mains sewerage is not an option the Mini Station d'épuration is often a viable alternative to the tradional fosse septique.

25 The Groves
Winchester
Hampshire
WR7 9PP

22nd March, 2006

Monsieur le Maire de Changé
53000 – CHANGE

Dear Mr Mayor,

### **Le Petit Bois 53000 Changé**

I wish to install a Mini sewage plant manufactured by Neve Environnement (a descriptive leaflet is enclosed)at the above property and I would ask your assistance as to whether this sewage disposal system meets with requirements of your department.

If this type of installation is permitted please let me have a list of surveyors who are approved by La Mairie to undertake the assessment and location of the installation.

Copies of the appropriate application form required would be appreciated.

Yours faithfully,

Gérard Broughton

Change the name of the manufacturer of the Mini Station d'épuration to your preferred supplier. You will probably find it easier to negotiate with the Mairie with a French manufacturer.

Gérard Broughton
25 The Groves
Winchester
Hampshire
WR7 9PP

Winchester, le 22 mars 2006

Monsieur le Maire de Changé
53000 – CHANGÉ

Monsieur le Maire,

**<u>Le Petit Bois 53000 Changé</u>**

J'ai l'intention d'installer une mini station d'épuration fabriquée par Neve Environnement (le descriptif est joint à cette lettre) dans la propriété citée en référence et aimerais avoir votre avis sur la validité de ce matériel dans le cadre de la réglementation sanitaire.

Si cette installation est autorisée veuillez avoir l'amabilité de me remettre une liste des entreprises agréées pour exécuter cette installation sous la surveillance du Service Sanitaire et de me faire parvenir le formulaire de demande d'autorisation.

Avec mes remerciements anticipés pour la bonne suite que vous voudrez bien apporter à ma demande, veuillez agréer, Monsieur le Maire, l'expression de mes sentiments les meilleurs.

Gérard Broughton

# Accept – Decline – Resign work position

Delete the unwanted salutation prefixes as required and remove brackets.
Remember to replace the date, time and job description as appropriate.

1

*Accept*

Dear (Sir \ Mr. Clements \ Mrs. Clements \ Ms Clements),

Thank you for your letter of 01\05\2006 offering me the post of English Teacher
It is with great pleasure that I accept this position and I confirm that I will be able to commence work on 10\05\2006 at 08.00  hours.

I look forward to working with your company and hope it will be beneficial to both of us.


Yours faithfully,


2

*Decline*

Thank you for your letter of 10\05\2006 offering me the post of  English Teacher

It is with great regret that I have to decline the position offered.

I hope that your company will soon find a suitable person for the position.


3

*Resign*

I wish to resign from my position of English Teacher .

My employment with this company will cease on 10\05\2006.

Replace the text of the acceptance letter outlined by arrows with decline or resign paragraphs as appropriate to the situation.

John Matthews
Le Petit Bois
Laval 53567

Laval, le 2 mai 2006

Monsieur (Madame \ Mademoiselle) Clements
Clavier Bricolage
Laval 53843

(Monsieur \ Monsieur Clements \ Madame Clements \ Mademoiselle Clements),

Je vous remercie de votre lettre du 01\05\2006 m'offrant le poste de professeur anglais

C'est avec grand plaisir que j'accepte votre proposition et vous confirme que je peux commencer le 10\05\2006 à 08.00 heures.

1

Je suis très heureux de travailler (avec vous \ ou dans votre Société) et espère vous donner satisfaction.

Veuillez agréer, (Monsieur \ Madame \ Mademoiselle), l'expression de mes sentiments distingués.

John Matthews

### *Decline*

Je vous remercie de votre lettre du 10\05\2006 m'offrant le poste de professeur anglais.
C'est avec regret que je décline votre proposition.

2

Je ne doute pas que vous trouverez quelqu'un intéressé par cette offre.

### *Resign*

Je souhaite cesser ma fonction de professeur anglais.

3

Mon emploi dans cette société cessera le 10\05\2006.

## Business Grants and Assistance

Unlike the UK where companies join the Chamber of Commerce and its business activities are not always in the forefront, in France it is an official government body responsible for business licensing and tax gathering. All businesses, large and small are known to them.

25 The Groves
Winchester
Hampshire
WR7 9PP

22nd March, 2006

The Chamber of Commerce and Industry
12, rue de Verdun
53000 LAVAL
France

Dear Sirs

I am considering transferring my business of (type of business) from (name of town and country) to (name of town) in ( 7 months).

Would you please advise me of what incentives and grants are available to businesses moving to this location and what assistance you are able to offer to facilitate such a move.

Yours faithfully,

John Clewis

The first place to start for business information in France is your Chamber of Commerce. Make sure to insert the type of business, location and date in the first paragraph and remove the brackets.

25 The Groves
Winchester
Hampshire
WR7 9PP

Winchester, le 22 mars 2006

Chambre de commerce et d'industrie
12, rue de Verdun
53000 Laval
France

Messieurs,

J'ai l'intention de transférer mon affaire de (type of business) de (name of town and country) à (name of town) dans ( 7 mois ).

Veuillez avoir l'obligeance de me faire connaître les aides, assistance et concessions accordées en cette matière tant pour le transfert que pour l'implantation.

Je vous en remercie bien vivement à l'avance et vous prie d'agréer, Messieurs, l'expression de mes sentiments distingués.

John Clewis

## Looking for Work or Training

Chambre de Commerce or Chambre de metiers for your town will be an excellent source of information on local businesses.

25 The Groves
Winchester
Hampshire
WR7 9PP

22nd March, 2006

The Chamber of Commerce and Industry
12, rue de Verdun
53000 Laval (France)

Dear Sirs

**1** I wish to work as a (Name of trade or profession) for which I am qualified and have 10 years experience.

Would you please advise me of other similar companies trading in the area of your responsibility.

**2** I wish to work as a (Name of trade or profession) for which I am qualified and have 10 years experience.

Would you please advise me of any suitable training courses you have available

Yours faithfully,

John Clewis

Fill in the name of your business or profession, change the number of years and remove the brackets.

25 The Groves
Winchester
Hampshire
WR7 9PP

Winchester, le 22 mars 2006

Chambre de commerce et d'industrie
12, rue de Verdun
53000 Laval  France

Messieurs,

(Name of trade or profession),qualifié\e, avec 10 années d'expérience, je suis à la recherche d'un emploi dans cette région.

Voudriez-vous avoir l'amabilité de me faire connaître le nom des sociétés dépendânt de votre autorité susceptibles d'être intéressées par ma demande?

| 1 |

(Name of trade or profession) qualifié\e, avec 10 années d'expérience, je suis à la recherche d'un emploi dans votre région.

Voudriez-vous avoir l'obligeance de me faire connaître les stages disponibles dans ma compétence?

| 2 |

Je vous en remercie bien vivement à l'avance.

Je vous prie d'agréer, Messieurs, l'expression de mes sentiments distingués.

John Clewis

## Job application to a company

Many jobs are not advertised and a speculative letter may be the way in to work.

---

Le Petit Bois
Laval 53567

2nd May, 2006

Monsanto
Place Centrale
Laval- 53500

Dear Sirs,

I am a qualified (architect \ craftsman \ beef farmer) with a degree in media studies.

My experience qualifies me to work efficiently in a company such as yours and you will see the relevance of my experience as you read my curriculum vitae I am looking for work in this region and I am writing to ask if you would consider employing me, preferably full time or perhaps part time?

Enclosed are references from previous employers, my curriculum vitae and a file of photographs showing projects I have worked on.

I would ask that you offer me the opportunity to meet you to discuss how I might be of value to your company.

Yours faithfully,

John Matthews

---

Replace your trade or profession and qualifications.

John Matthews
Le Petit Bois
Laval 53567

Laval, le 2 mai 2006

Monsanto
Place Centrale
Laval- 53500

Messieurs,

Je possède une formation (d'architecte \ d'artisan \ d'agriculteur), je suis titulaire d'un diplôme en études de médias.

Mon expérience m'a permis de travailler efficacement dans une compagnie semblable à la vôtre et vous pourrez en juger en lisant mon curriculum vitae; je désirerais travailler dans cette région et vous demande, par cette lettre, si vous pouvez envisager un emploi pour moi de préférence à plein temps ou éventuellement à mi-temps?

Je joins à cette lettre les références de mes précédents employeurs, mon curriculum vitae et des photos des projets que j'ai réalisés.

Puis-je solliciter une entrevue pour discuter de mon éventuelle contribution au sein de votre compagnie?

Avec mes remerciements anticipés pour l'étude que vous voudrez bien faire de mon dossier.

Veuillez agréer, Messieurs, l'expression de mes sentiments distingués.

John Matthews

## Apply for an advertised job

Le Petit Bois
Laval 53567

2nd May, 2006

Clavier Bricolage
Rue de rive mayenne
Laval- 53500

Dear Sirs,

I have seen your advertisement in the Mayenne Courier, page 29, 02\05\2006 and I think my experience and qualifications as a (builder \baker \ public relations consultant) with a degree in media studies make me suitable for this position.

My experience qualifies me to work efficiently in a company such as yours and you will see the relevance of my experience as you read my curriculum vitae I am looking for work in this region and I am writing to ask if you would consider employing me, preferably full time or perhaps part time?

Enclosed are reference from previous employers, my curriculum vitae and a file of photographs showing projects I have worked on.

I would ask that you offer me the opportunity to meet you to discuss how I might be of value to your company.

Yours faithfully,


John Matthews

Replace the newspaper, page number, date, degree and occupation to fit your situation. They are in the same order in both languages.

John Matthews
Le Petit Bois
Laval 53567

Laval, le 2 mai 2006

Clavier Bricolage
Rue de rive mayenne
Laval- 53500

Messieurs,

J'ai lu votre annonce dans le Courrier de la Mayenne du 02\05\2006, page 29 et je pense que mon expérience et mes diplômes de (maçon\ boulanger \ conseil en relations publiques) ainsi que ma licence en sciences de communication font de moi un candidat idéal à ce poste.

Mon expérience m'a permis de travailler efficacement dans une compagnie semblable à la vôtre et vous pourrez en juger en lisant mon curriculum vitae; je désirerais travailler dans cette région et vous demande, par cette lettre, si vous pouvez envisager un emploi pour moi de préférence à plein temps ou éventuellement à mi-temps?

Je joins à cette lettre les références de mes précédents employeurs, mon curriculum vitae et des photos des projets que j'ai mis en oeuvre.

Puis-je solliciter une entrevue afin de discuter de mon éventuelle contribution au sein de votre compagnie?

Avec mes remerciements anticipés pour l'étude que vous voudrez bien faire de mon dossier, veuillez agréer, Messieurs, l'expression de mes sentiments distingués.

John Matthews

# Register for work with the Chambre de Metiers

Self employment is not as simple as the U.K. The list of taxes and contributions is horrendous but do not be tempted to work "on the black". The penalties are far worse than the taxes!

Les PetitsBois
53501 - LAVAL

22nd August, 2006

Chambre des Métiers
Place du 11 Novembre
35300 – LAVAL

Dear Sirs

I wish to commence work as a (Name of trade or profession) for which I am qualified and have 10 years experience.

Would you please advise me of the registration procedure and all the cotisations and the payment structures that are involved.

Please ensure that details are sent of charges to URSSAF (sociale sécurité), ASSEDIC (unemployment) AVA (retirement and death); PROBTP (retirement and health),Taxe Professionnelle (commune charge).

I will also require Résponsabilité Déçenéle (10 year work guarantee) & Civile (public liability) and need names of companies approved for this insurance.

Yours faithfully,

Gérard Broughton

Insert your trade or profession in the bracketed area and remove the brackets. Don't forget to change the period of experience to your own.

Gérard et Marion BROUGHTON
Les Petit Bois
53501 - LAVAL

Laval, le 22 août 2006

> Chambre des Métiers
> Place du 11 Novembre
> 35300 - LAVAL

Monsieur,

Etant titulaire d'un diplôme de (*Name of trade or profession*) avec 10 ans d'expérience, je suis à la recherche d'un emploi.

Veuillez avoir l'amabilité de me faire connaître la procédure d'inscription, toutes les côtisations et le salaire pratiqué pour mon cas.

Pourriez-vous aussi me faire parvenir le détail des charges à régler à : l'URSSAF, l'ASSEDIC, l'Assurance retraite et décès, l'Assurance retraite et santé, la taxe professionnelle ou autres.

Je voudrais également m'assurer en Responsabilité Décénale et Civile et connaître les Compagnies d'assurances adéquates.

Avec mes remerciements anticipés pour votre réponse, veuillez agréer, Monsieur, l'expression de mes meilleurs sentiments.

Gérard Broughton

## Simple CV

This one you have to write yourself – but it is a common style in France.

**CLEMENTS, Phillip John**
**Adresse:**
*Le Petit Bois*
*Laval 53567*

Tél.:                   *Your data*
Date of Birth:    *Your data*
Marital Status:   *Your data*
Nationality:       *Your data*
**Education**
*College\University name: Qualification*

*Date*
*College*
*A Levels:*

*Dates*
*School*
*GCSEs*

**Work Experience**
*Date*
*Description of work experience*

*Date*
*Description of work experience*

**Interests**
*At School:*

*College\University*

*Present*

**Other Information**

*List any activities you have been involved with*
*Voluntary work*
*Other activities*

If it is in italics you need to replace it with your own information. Keep it simple the longer the CV, the more room for language errors.

If it is in italics you need to replace it with your own information. Keep it simple the longer the CV, the more room for language errors.

***Phillip , John Clements***
**Adresse**

*Le Petit Bois*
*Saint Mania de Mans*
*64530 - MAYBELLE*

| | |
|---|---|
| Tel: | *Your data* |
| Date de Naissance | *Your data* |
| Régime matrimonial | *Your data* |
| Nationalité | *Your data* |

**Formation**
*Lycée\ Université name* - formation

*Dates*
*Lycée*
*A. Levels\ Baccalauréat:*

*Dates*
*Collège*
*GCSEs\ Brevet des collèges*

**Expérience professionnelle**

*Date*
*Description du travail effectué ( ou de la responsabilité )*

*Date*
*Description du travail effectué ( ou de la responsabilité )*

**Activités extra-scolaires**

**Au collège**

*Au lycée \à l'université*

**Autres informations**

*Permis de conduire*
Liste des autres activités que vous avez pu exercer
dans un travail bénévole
Autres activités

# Car exhaust - replace or repair

Unlikely you would ever write this letter in the UK but you might need it to explain what work you want done at a repair centre.

Les Petits-Bois
53872 - LAVAL

12<sup>th</sup> April, 2006

Dear Sirs,

### Vehicle Registration No: MU 51 DGH

The above vehicle requires the exhaust system to be checked and repaired or replaced as required.

Please advise of the cost and a suitable date and time you require the vehicle and the time it will be available for collection.

The above vehicle requires the (front exhaust pipe \ front exhaust box \ middle exhaust box \ rear exhaust box \ catalytic converter) to be replaced.

Please advise of the cost and time it will be available for collection.

Yours faithfully,

Gerald Clements

Repair or Replace

Components

Tyre and Exhaust companies are the same in France as the UK – a sharp intake of breath and a shaking head. Pin down what you want done by selecting the appropriate choices; they are in the same order as the English version

---

Gerald Clements
Les Petits-Bois
53872 - LAVAL

Laval, le 12 avril 2006

Vulco Mayenne
225 La Peyennière
53100 MAYENNE

Monsieur,

### Véhicule Immatriculé no MU 51 DGH

Le système d'échappement de mon véhicule référencé ci-dessus présente des problèmes et demande à être vérifié et réparé ou remplacé suivant le cas.

Veuillez me faire connaître le détail et le coût des travaux que vous jugez nécessaires, la date à laquelle vous pouvez intervenir et le temps nécessaire.

Avec mes remerciements anticipés ainsi que mes sentiments les meilleurs.

Repair or Replace

Le système d'échappement de mon véhicule cité en reférence présente des problèmes au (niveau \ tuyau d'echappement \ tête d'échappement \ pot d'échappement \ pot catalyseur).

Veuillez m'en faire connaître le coût et le temps prévu pour cettre intervention.

Avec mes remerciements anticipés ainsi que mes meilleurs sentiments.

Components

Gerald Clements

---

# Change Tyres and Puncture repairs

A routine but essential car chore.

---

Le Petit Bois
Laval 53567

2nd October, 2006

Dear Sirs,

## Vehicle Registration No: MU 51 CDH

The above vehicle requires tyres size  560 x 15 x 150 to the
(front nearside) (front offside)
(rear nearside) rear offside)

Please advise of the cost and a suitable date and time you require the vehicle and
the time it will be available for collection.

Yours faithfully,

Dear Sirs,

## Vehicle Registration No: MU 51 CDH

Please repair the puncture to the wheel supplied.

Please advise of the time it will be available for collection.

Yours faithfully,

Gerald Clements

---

Select the tyres to be replaced and change the tyre size to the correct one for your car.

Le Petit Bois
Laval 53567

Laval, le 2 octobre 2006

Vulco Mayenne
225 La Peyennière
53100 MAYENNE

Messieurs,

### No Immatriculation Véhicule MU 51 CDH

Ce véhicule a besoin d'un changement de pneu(s) de dimension 560x 15 x 150 à
(l'avant gauche)   (l'avant droit)
(l'arrière gauche )   (l'arrière droit ).

Veuillez me faire connaître le prix et me dire quel jour et à quelle heure je dois vous amener ce véhicule ainsi que le temps d'attente.

Avec mes remerciements anticipés, veuillez recevoir, Messieurs, mes meilleures salutations.

Change Tyres

Messieurs,

### No Immatriculation Véhicule: MU 51 CDH

La roue de ce véhicule est crevée; voudriez-vous avoir l'obligeance de la réparer.

Veuillez m'informer également de la durée que nécessite une telle intervention.

Avec mes remerciements anticipés, veuillez recevoir, Messieurs, mes meilleures salutations.

Puncture

Gerald Clements

## Wheel Balance and Alignment

Sometimes it is easier to say what you want in a note rather than struggle with technical terms in French.

25 The Groves
Winchester
Hampshire
WR7 9PP

22nd March, 2006

Euromaster
r Marie André Ampère
ZI de la Peyenneire
53100 Mayenne

Dear Sirs,

### Vehicle Registration No: AS53 ABC

The above vehicle requires the wheels to be balanced to the (front nearside \ front offside \ rear nearside\ rear offside).

The above vehicle requires the wheel alignment to be checked and adjusted as required.

Please advise of the cost and a suitable date and time you require the vehicle and the time it will be available for collection.

Yours faithfully,

Gérard Broughton

Garages tend to be the same the world over – put it in writing and there can't be any argument about what you want.

Gérard Broughton
25 The Groves
Winchester
Hampshire
WR7 9PP

Winchester, le 22 mars 2006

Euromaster
r Marie André Ampère
ZI de la Peyenneire
53100 Mayenne

Monsieur,

### *Véhicule immatriculé : AS53 ABC*

Je vous serais reconnaissant de rééquilibrer les roues de cette voiture (avant gauche \ avant droite \ arrière gauche \ arrière droite).

Voudriez vous vérifier et éventuellement, ajuster l'alignement des roues de ce véhicule?

Veuillez m'en donner le coût et le temps d'intervention afin que je puisse prendre mes dispositions; veuillez également me donner la date d'intervention.

Avec mes remerciements anticipés ainsi que mes sentiments les meilleurs.

Gérard Broughton

Wheel Balance

Alignment

# Replace Lost or Stolen Driving Licence

Having finally obtained a French driving licence you may just be unfortunate enough to lose it! All is not lost – first report the loss in person to the police station or the gendamerie unit. You will be given an official receipt, which is valid as a driving licence for two months. During this time you must apply for a duplicate at the Prefecture of your place of residence. You will need the documents listed in the letter. You will probably have to pay a fee but a few regions do not charge. Apply in person if possible – the replacement is normally issued immediately.

Les Petits Bois
53501 - LAVAL

22nd August, 2006

The Prefecture,
46, rue Mazagran
53015 – LAVAL  CEDEX

Dear Sirs,

### <u>Replacement Driving Licence</u>

I have lost my driving licence and I would ask that you issue me with a replacement.

Enclosed are the required documents:

> 3 passport photographs
> Receipt for declaration of loss
> My passport

Please advise me of the fee required for the replacement.

Yours faithfully,

Marion Broughton

One of those letters that it is better to deliver personally. Passports should never be posted unless it is absolutely unavoidable . Check the correct address for your area with the mairie or yellow pages.

Marion BROUGHTON
Les Petits Bois
53501 - LAVAL

Laval le 22 Août 2006

Préfecture de la Mayenne
46 rue Mazagran
53015 - LAVAL CEDEX

Monsieur le Préfet,

J'ai perdu mon permis de conduire et vous serais reconnaissant de vouloir bien m'en délivrer un duplicata

Je joins à ce pli les documents suivants:

3 photos d'identité

Le récépissé de la déclaration de perte

Mon passeport.

Voudriez-vous me faire connaitre le coût de ce nouveau document, et les pièces supplémentaires nécessaires que j'aurais omis de joindre à ce pli?

Avec mes remerciements anticipés, veuillez agréer, Monsieur le Préfet, l'expression de mes sentiments distingués.

Marion BROUGHTON

# Forms and Documents to exchange driving licence.

Regulations change rapidly and it may be worth enquiring before sending in documents.

Les Petits-Bois
53872 - LAVAL

12<sup>th</sup> April, 2006

La Préfecture
53510  Laval

Dear Sirs,

I wish to change my United Kingdom driving licence to a French driving licence and request that you send me form:

Cerfa n°11247*01 demande d'échange de permis de conduire.

Please advise me of all documents required and the fee required for the exchange

Yours faithfully,

Gerald Clements

Just look up the address of the Prefecture and send this letter to get the forms and list of documents.

---

Gerald Clements
Les Petits-Bois
3872 - LAVAL

Laval, le 12 avril 2006

La Préfecture
53510 Laval

Monsieur le Préfet,

J'ai l'intention d'échanger mon permis de conduire anglais pour un permis français et je vous serais reconnaissant de bien vouloir m'adresser le formulaire Cerfa no 11247 *01 de demande d'échange de permis de conduire.

Veuillez me donner la liste de tous les documents requis et le montant du réglement en pareille matière.

Je vous en remercie vivement à l'avance.

Veuillez agréer, Monsieur le Préfet, l'expression de ma haute considération.

Gerald Clements

# Exchange UK driving Licence for French Licence

It is advisable to take this letter and documents rather than risk losing them in the post. Official translations are normally required.

Les Petits-Bois
53872 - LAVAL

12<sup>th</sup> April, 2006

La Préfecture
53510 Laval


Dear Sirs,

I wish to change my United Kingdom driving licence to a French driving licence and enclose the following documents:

Form Cerfa n°11247*01 demande d'échange de permis de conduire
Original United Kingdom driving licence   *(You may require an official translation)*
Passport
Carte de séjour        *(both sides must be copied)*
EDF, GDF or water bill      *(One only as proof of residence)*
Proof of no driving bans or restrictions
2 photographs  3.5 cm x 3.5 cm
An additional set of photocopies of all of the above documents
€25 fee for exchange of licence. *( Check the correct fee)*


Yours faithfully,


Gerald Clements.

Make sure all documents and copies are enclosed and the correct fee inserted.

---

Gerald Clements
Les Petits-Bois
53872 - LAVAL

Laval, le 12 avril 2006

La Préfecture
53510 Laval

Monsieur le Préfet,

Je souhaiterais échanger mon permis de conduire anglais pour un permis français et je joins à ce pli les documents suivants:

Formulaire **Cerfa no11247\*01** de demande d'échange de permis de conduire
Mon permis de conduire UK original
Mon passeport
Ma carte de séjour ou permis de résidence
Facture de ( EDF \ GDF \ d'EAU)
Certificat de non interdiction ou de restriction de conduire.
2 photos 3,5 cm x 3,5cm
Les photocopies de tous les documents originaux ci-joints.
25 Euros en réglement des droits d'échange de permis. *( Check the correct fee)*

Recevez mes remerciements anticipés pour la bonne suite que vous voudrez bien apporter à mon dossier.

Veuillez agréer, Monsieur le Préfet, l'expression de ma haute considération.


Gerald Clements

# Motor Insurance quotation

Motor insurers in France may ask for proof of no accidents or claims for as long as ten years.

---

Le Petit Bois
Laval 53567

2nd May, 2006

Hérivaux Assureur
86, rue Victor Boissel
B.P.0816
53008 LAVAL Cedex

Dear Sirs,

### <u>Volvo V40 2004  MU54YNT</u>

I require motor insurance for the above vehicle with the following specification:

| | |
|---|---|
| Owner: | Name |
| age | sex |
| marital status | occupation |
| No claims bonus: | 12 years |
| Cover required: | (Comprehensive) (Third party fire and theft) |
| Convictions: | (none \ List convictions and dates, points) |
| Type of Licence: | (Full \ Provisional)   3 Points on Licence |
| Number of years Driving: | 27 |

| | |
|---|---|
| **Other driver** | Name |
| Age | Sex |
| Marital status | Occupation |
| Type of Licence: | (Full \ Provisional)  0 Points on Licence |
| Number of years Driving: | 10 |
| Accident record: | (None \ Date, claim value) |

**Other named driver**:          *(Repeat above details for all other drivers)*

Please let me have your quotation.

Yours faithfully,


John Matthews

---

Please take great care with any insurance details – inaccurate information, even accidentally may invalidate a policy.

---

Le Petit Bois
Laval 53567

Laval, le 2 mai 2006

                                Hérivaux Assureur
                                86, rue Victor Boissel
                                B.P.0816
                                53008 LAVAL Cedex

Messieurs,

<u>Volvo V40 2004  MU54YNT</u>

Je désire assurer le véhicule cité en référence dont voici les renseignements:

**Propriétaire:**

| | |
|---|---|
| Age: | Sexe: |
| Situation familiale | Profession: |
| Pas d'accident: | 12ans |
| Couverture demandée | (Etendue \Tiers collision, incendie, vol, bris de glace) |
| Condamnation | (Aucune\ *List convictions etc*) |
| Permis de conduire | (plein \ provisoire) 3 points |
| Nombre d'années de conduite | 27 |

| | |
|---|---|
| **Autre conducteur** | Nom, âge etc |
| Permis de conduire | (plein \ provisoire) 0 points |
| Nombre d'années de conduite | 10 |
| Accidents enregistrés | (Aucun \ *Date, claim value*) |
| Autre conducteur: | |

Veuillez me faire une proposition de prix.

Avec mes remerciements anticipés, veuillez agréer, Messieurs, l'expression de mes sentiments distingués.

John Matthews

## Attestation de Conformité

Without this certificate you will be unable to change your vehicle registration from UK to French.

Les Petits Bois
53501 - LAVAL

22nd August, 2006

Insert the name and Address of
the car manufacturer's head office in France.
If you have difficulty, the UK or French
dealership network may be able to help.

Dear Sirs

### Vehicle: Volvo, Model V70 UK Registration MU51KIT

### Attestation de conformité

Dear Sirs,

I require an attestation de conformite for the above vehicle. Please inform me of the documentation you require to issue this.

Yours faithfully,

Gérard Broughton

A very simple letter but a vital piece of documentation! The address must be the manufacturers headquarters, normally in France, not a dealership.

Gérard et Marion BROUGHTON
Les Petits Bois
53501 - LAVAL

Laval, le 22 août 2006

Volvo
Place de la Concorde
31245 - PARIS

Messieurs,

### *Véhicule : Volvo , Modèle V70    IMMATRICULÉ UK : MU51KIT*

### *Attestation de Conformité*

J'ai besoin d'une attestation de conformité pour le véhicule cité en référence. Voudriez-vous me dire quelles sont les formalités à remplir pour obtenir une telle attestation?

Avec mes remerciements anticipés pour la bonne suite que vous voudrez bien apporter à ma demande,veuillez agréer, Messieurs, l'expression de mes sentiments distingués.

Gérard Broughton

# Certificat de dédouanement

Take this letter **DO NOT POST IT** documents have a habit of going astray when they are this important

Les Petits Bois
53501 - LAVAL

22nd August, 2006

Centre des impôts
Hotel des Finances
60 Rue Macdonald
LAVAL
53090 LAVAL Cedex 9

Dear Sirs

### Vehicle: Volvo, Model V70  UK Registration MU51KIT

Enclosed are originals of the vehicle's United Kingdom registration papers and sales receipt showing payment of VAT.

Would you please issue the Certificat de dédouanement 846A for the vehicle to be registered in France.

Yours faithfully,

Gérard et Marion Broughton

Gérard et Marion BROUGHTON
Les Petits Bois
53501 - LAVAL


Laval, le 22 août 2006


Centre des impôts
Hotel des Finances
60 Rue Macdonald
LAVAL
53090 LAVAL Cedex 9


Monsieur le Directeur,

### Véhicule: Volvo, Modèle V70, Immatriculation anglaise MU51KIT

Sous ce pli veuillez trouver les documents d'immatriculation en Angleterre de ce véhicule ainsi qu'un reçu indiquant le montant des taxes payées.

Veuillez me délivrer le certificat de dédouanement 846A pour que ce véhicule soit immatriculé en France.

Avec mes remerciements anticipés, veuillez agréer, Monsieur le Directeur, l'expression de mes sentiments distingués.


Marion Broughton

# Register UK car in France

Registration of your car will only be difficult if you try to omit any of the documents listed.

---

Les Petits Bois
53501 - LAVAL

22nd August, 2006

**Préfecture or Sous Préfecture
for your town or area – Get
the address from phone
directory or the Mairie**

Dear Sirs,

**<u>Demande d'immatriculation</u>
<u>Vehicle: Volvo, Model V70 UK Registration MU51KIT</u>**

Enclosed are the following documents:

> Passport or Carte de Séjour
> Electricity, phone or water bill
> UK Vehicle registration document
> Attestation of Conformité
> Certificat de dédouanement 846A
> Contrôle Technique certificate (if vehicle is over 4 years old)

Please notify me when I should return for the Carte Grise.

Yours faithfully

Marion Broughton

---

Probably wise to make a special journey with document as valuable as these.

Marion BROUGHTON
Les Petits Bois
53501 - LAVAL

Laval, le 22 août 2006

**Préfecture or Sous Préfecture
For your town or area – Get
the address from phone
directory or the Mairie**

Monsieur le Préfet,

*__Demande d'immatriculation du véhicule__*
*__Marque Volvo Modèle V70, UK Numéro d'immatriculation__*
**MU51KIT**

Veuillez trouver sous ce pli les documents suivants:

Passeport ou Carte de Séjour
Facture (électricité, téléphone ou eau)
Document d'immatriculation anglaise du véhicule
Attestation de conformité
Certificat de dédouanement
Attestation du contrôle technique

Veuillez avoir l'obligeance de me faire savoir à quelle date ma carte grise
sera prête.

Je vous remercie à l'avance et vous prie d'agréer, Monsieur le Préfet,
l'expression de ma haute considération.

Marion Broughton

# Request car service and estimate

A simple request but a letter clarifies what you want until your language skills enable you to make your own arrangements verbally.

Les Petit Bois
53501 - LAVAL

22nd August, 2006

Euromaster
r Marie André Ampère
ZI de la Peyenneire
53100 Mayenne

Dear Sirs,

**<u>Vehicle Registration No: AS53 ABC</u>**

The above vehicle requires servicing according to manufacturers requirements for a 30,000 (mile \ Km) service.

Please advise of the cost and a suitable date and time you require the vehicle and the time it will be available for collection.

Please service the above vehicle according to manufacturers requirements for a Volvo V70 30,000 (mile \ Km) service.

Please advise of the time it will be available for collection.

Yours faithfully,

Gérard  Broughton

Each of the marked paragraphs is a separate letter, select the one relevant to yourself and change the mileage and insert the make and model accordingly.

Gérard BROUGHTON
Les Petit Bois
53501 - LAVAL

laval, le 22 août 2006

Euromaster
r Marie André Ampère
ZI de la Peyenneire
53100 Mayenne

Monsieur,

### Véhicule immatriculé No: AS53 ABC

Le véhicule ci-dessus référencé (Marque – Modèle) doit être revisé suivant le carnet de garantie de la firme automobile au stade des 30000 (miles \ kms ).

Veuillez m'en faire connaître le coût, la date à laquelle vous pourrez intervenir ainsi que le temps nécessaire à ce contrôle.

Pourriez-vous réviser la voiture citée en référence de marque Volvo et modèle V70 qui ayant atteint les 30000 (miles \ kms ) nécessite un contrôle technique.

Veuillez m'aviser du temps nécessaire pour cette révision.

Recevez mes remerciements anticipés ainsi que mes meilleurs sentiments.

Gérard Broughton

Arrange a Service

Take for Service

# Inform Doctor of Medical Conditions

Medical records are important and need to be available to give to the new doctor as soon as possible.

Le Petit Bois
Laval 53567

$2^{nd}$ May, 2006

Dr Pasteur,
132 Boulevard Sierre
LAVAL

Dear Dr Pasteur,

When we met we discussed (my \ Jeanette Clewens) medical condition and I have obtained copies of the doctors records from the UK and I enclose them.

Please let me know if you wish to see (me \ Jeanette Clewens) again regarding this matter.

Yours faithfully,

Peter Clewens

Select the correct person and insert the name where appropriate.

Le Petit Bois
Laval 53567


Laval, le 2 mai 2006


                                        Dr Pasteur,
                                        132 Boulevard Sierre
                                        LAVAL



Cher Docteur,

Suite à notre rencontre et à notre discussion au sujet (de mon état de santé\ de
l'état de santé de Jeannette Clewens ) j'ai obtenu  les dossiers médicaux de
l'Angleterre que je vous ai adressés.

Veuillez avoir l'amabilité de me faire savoir si vous voulez (me revoir \ revoir
Jeanette Clewens) au sujet de ce document?

Avec mes remerciements anticipés, veuillez agréer, cher Docteur, l'expression de
mes meilleurs sentiments.



Peter Clewens

## CPAM leaflet on Health Insurance Integration

CPAM publish an excellent leaflet in English on changing from the UK health service to the French system.

Les Petits Bois
53501 - LAVAL

22nd August, 2006

Caisse Primaire d'assurance maladie
Rue du Général De Gaulle
53012 LAVAL Cedex

Dear Sirs,

(I \ We) wish to change our health registration to France.

Would you be kind enough to let (me \ us)  have a copy of your information leaflet "How can a socially insured person from a member country of the European Economic Area benefit from the French Social Security System" Together with the appropriate forms to obtain a social security number and Carte Vitale.

Yours faithfully,

Gérard and Marion Broughton

You will need to look up the correct address for your nearest CPAM (Caisse Primaire d'Assurance Maladie) office. It will be in yellow pages or the local mairie will give you the address.

Gérard et Marion BROUGHTON
Les Petits Bois
53501 - LAVAL

Laval, le 22 août 2006

Caisse Primaire d'assurance maladie
Rue du Général De Gaulle
53012 LAVAL Cedex

Monsieur le Directeur,

(Je souhaiterais \ Nous souhaiterions) modifier notre régime de santé en accord avec celui existant en France.

Veuillez avoir l'amabilité de (m'adresser \ nous adresser) un exemplaire de la documentation relative aux personnes membres d'un Pays de la Zone Economique Européenne désirant bénéficier du régime français de sécurité sociale? Pourriez-vous y joindre également le formulaire adéquat pour l'obtention du No d'inscription à ce régime ainsi que la carte vitale.

Avec (mes \ nos) remerciements anticipés pour la réponse que vous voudrez bien (me \ nous) faire, veuillez agréer, Monsieur le Directeur, l'expression de (mes \ nos) sentiments distingués.

Gérard et Marion BROUGHTON

## Register with a doctor or Dentist

Finding a doctor or dentist is probably easier in France. Your neighbours may make a recommendation or the mairie will give you a list of practitioners.

---

Les Petit Bois
53501 - LAVAL

22nd August, 2006

Cabinet Laval
192 Rue de Pascal
53500 – LAVAL

Dear Sir,

(I \ We) will be moving to the above address on 05\11\2006) \ (I \ We) have moved to the above address) and would like to register as a patient with you as soon as possible.

(I \ We) have copies of my (medical \dental) records from the UK and would like an appointment with you to discuss ongoing treatment.

(I \ We) do not have any (medical \ dental) records from the UK but (I \ we) would like to make an appointment to introduce (myself \ ourselves).

Yours faithfully

Gérard and Marion Broughton

---

Be careful to select the paragraph with medical \ dental records or without and change the date to suit your situation.

Gérard et Marion BROUGHTON
Les Petit Bois
53501 - LAVAL

Laval, le 22 août 2006

Cabinet Laval
192 Rue de Pascal
53500 - LAVAL

Cher Docteur,

(J'ai \ Nous avons) l'intention d'habiter à l'adresse ci-dessus le 05\11\2006) \ ( J'habite \ Nous habitons ) à l'adresse ci-dessus et (voudrais \ voudrions) prendre rendez-vous à votre cabinet le plus tôt possible.

Records

(J'ai \ Nous avons) obtenu les résultats de (ma \ notre) situation (médicale \ dentaire) suite aux examens et soins pratiqués en Angleterre et (je voudrais \ nous voudrions) en discuter avec vous pour poursuivre le traitement.

No Records

(Je suis \ Nous sommes) dans l'impossibilité de vous fournir un carnet de soin ou des résultats d' examen (dentaires) en provenance de l'Angleterre. Cependant,(je souhaiterais \ nous souhaiterions) prendre un rendez- vous afin de vous rencontrer.

En attendant ce rendez-vous, veuillez agréer, cher Docteur, l'expression de (ma \ notre) considération distinguée.

Gérard et Marion Broughton

# List of Schools Public and Private

The mayor of your town or village is an excellent source of information

Le Petit Bois
53567 Laval

2 May, 2006

Monsieur Le Maire
La Mairie
Laval 53843

Dear Sirs

(I \ We) will be moving to your town (village \ city)  on 20\09\2006.

Is it possible for the mayor's office to provide a list of  (primary schools \ nurseries \ secondary schools \ colleges) that serve the area?

(I \ We) would like both state and private organisations to be included in the list

Yours faithfully,

John  and Mary Matthews

Edit the letter to include the type of schools you are looking for.

| maternelles | = | nursery |
| primaires | = | primary |
| secondaires | = | secondary |

Remove the singular \ plural as required

Le Petit Bois
53567 Laval

Laval, le 2 mai 2006

Monsieur le Maire
LAVAL
53300 - LAVAL

Objet : Liste des établissements scolaires.

Monsieur le Maire,

(Je dois \ Nous devons) emménager dans votre (ville \ village) le 20\09\2006.

Voudriez-vous avoir l'obligeance de me faire parvenir la liste des écoles maternelles, primaires et secondaires, tant du secteur public que du secteur privé des alentours.

(Je vous en remercie \ Nous vous en remercions) vivement à l'avance.

Veuillez agréer, cher Monsieur, l'expression de (mes \ nos) meilleurs sentiments.

John et Mary Matthews

# Enrol Children for Ecole Maternelle

Ecoles Maternelles for children under 6 years of age. The school is normally free of charge but there may be extras such as lunch.

---

Les Petits-Bois
53872 - LAVAL

12<sup>th</sup> April, 2006

Les Petits-Bois
53872 - LAVAL

12th April, 2006


La Mairie
53501 LAVAL


Dear Mr. Mayor,

(I \ We) understand that enrolment for Écoles Maternelles is at the Mairie. It is (my \ our) wish to enrol my (child \ children)

| | |
|---|---|
| Maximillan Clements | aged 2 year 10 months |
| Maxine Clements | aged 3 year 7 months |
| Peter Clements | aged 5 year 1 month |

(I \ We) have doctor's certificates for the children showing (their \ his \ her) vaccination dates for the following:

Combined mumps measles and ruebella
BCG   (mandatory)

Would you please supply me with any forms that are required and inform me of any extra charges that are made.


Yours faithfully,


Gerald and Marion Clements

---

Just edit to fit your family names

Les Petits-Bois
53872 - LAVAL

Laval, le 12 avril, 2006

La Mairie
53501 LAVAL

Monsieur le Maire,

(J'ai \ Nous avons) appris que l'inscription pour l'école maternelle se faisait en Mairie.

(Je désire \ Nous désirons) y inscrire (mon \ notre) enfant ( mes \ nos enfants ) :

| | |
|---|---|
| Maximillan Clements | âgé de 2 ans et 10 mois |
| Maxine Clements | âgée de 3 ans et 7 mois |
| Peter Clements | âgé de 5 ans et 1 mois. |

(Je tiens \ Nous tenons) à votre disposition (le certificat de vaccination  délivré \ les certificats de vaccination  délivrés) par le médecin .

Vaccin oreillons - rougeole et rubéole
BCG

Voudriez-vous avoir l'amabilité de (me \ nous) faire parvenir les documents à remplir et de (me \ nous) renseigner sur les frais éventuels à régler.

Avec (mes \ nos) remerciements anticipés, veuillez agréer, Monsieur le Maire, l'expression de (mes \ nos) meilleurs sentiments.

Gerald et Marion Clements

# Get school details and brochure

Change the dates and insert the appropriate name(s) as required. Some vaccination certificates are mandatory.

---

Les Petits Bois<br>
53501 - LAVAL

22nd August, 2006

The Headteacher,
Ecole Louis VX
Rue St Bernard
Laval

Dear Sirs,

(My \ Our) family will be moving to this area soon on 23\09\2006 and I am considering your school for (my child, Julia aged 12 \ my children ,Julia age 12, Paul age 14, and Patricia age 16).

(I \ We) have doctor's certificates for the children showing (our child's \ our children's) vaccination dates for Tuberculosis (BCG) and Diphtheria-Tetanus-Polio (DTP).

Would you please have a copy of the school prospectus sent to (me \ us) together with a note of the fees and uniform requirements.

Perhaps you would be kind enough to contact (me \ us) to arrange for (me \ us) to visit the school when we could discuss their academic and language skills.

Yours faithfully,

Gérard and Marion Broughton

Careful with the male \ female headteacher alternatives and keep count of the name(s).

Gérard et Marion BROUGHTON
Les Petits Bois
53501 - LAVAL


Laval, le 22 août 2006

(Monsieur le Directeur \ Madame la Directrice )
Ecole Louis VX
Rue St Bernard
Laval

(Monsieur le Directeur \ Madame la Directrice),

(Ma \ Notre) famille va emménager dans votre région le 23\09\2006 et j'ai choisi votre établissement pour (mon enfant Julia âgée de 12 ans\ pour mes enfants – Julia âgée de 12 ans, Paul âgé de 14 ans, et Patricia âgée de 16 ans).

(Je posséde \ Nous possédons) les certificats du Médecin certifiant que notre (enfant a reçu \ nos enfants ont reçu) les vaccinations de la tuberculose (BCG) et de la diphtérie-tétanos-polio (DTP).

Voudriez-vous avoir l'amabilité de m'adresser une documentation sur votre ecole ainsi que le tarif trimestriel et éventuellement, l'uniforme requis.

(Je vous serai \ Nous vous serions) très reconnaissants de bien vouloir nous accorder un rendez-vous afin de visiter votre établissement et de discuter du niveau scolaire de (notre enfant \ nos enfants) ainsi que de (sa \ leur) capacité linguistique.

Avec (mes \ nos) remerciements anticipés,veuillez agréer, (Monsieur le Directeur \ Madame la Directrice ) l'expression de (mes \ nos) sentiments distingués.


Gérard et Marion Broughton.

## Starting School and School records

Take care with the options – they are in the same order in English and French.

Les Petits Bois
53501 - LAVAL

22nd August, 2006

Collège Jacques Monod
45 bd Frédéric Chaplet
53000 LAVAL

Dear Sirs,

Thank you for agreeing to accept my (child \ children), Mary and Peter at your (secondary school \ primary school \ nursery).

I enclose a copy of the records I have been given from (his \ her \ their) school in the U.K.

They will commence at the school on 01\10\2006 and (I \ we) will accompany them to the school and report to the (school \ nursery) office at 08.30 hours.

Yours faithfully,

Gérard and Marion Broughton

Take care with the sentence starting commencera \commenceront it gets slightly complicated.

---

Gérard et Marion BROUGHTON
Les Petits Bois
53501 - LAVAL

Laval, le 22 août 2006

Collège Jacques Monod
45 bd Frédéric Chaplet
53000 LAVAL

(Monsieur le Directeur \ Madame la Directrice ,

Nous vous remercions de bien vouloir accepter (notre enfant \ nos enfants) Mary et Peter à votre (école \ école maternelle \ crèche).

Veuillez trouver sous ce pli le dossier scolaire qui (lui a été donné \ leur a été donné) par l'école Anglaise.

| Male | Female | Male or mixed sex plural | Female Plural |
|------|--------|--------------------------|---------------|

(Il commencera \ Elle commencera \ Ils commenceront \ Elles commenceront ) l'école le 01\10\2006 et je (l'y accompagnerai \ les y accompagnerai ) et me présenterai à l'accueil de votre ( école \ maternelle \ crèche ) à 08.30 heures.

Veuillez agréer, (Monsieur le Directeur \ Madame la Directrice ) l'expression de mes sentiments les meilleurs.

Gérard et Marion Broughton

---

## Arrange visit to School

Courtesy requires that you ask to visit a school before making any decision or visit. The mairie will be happy to let you have lists of state and private schools.

25 The Groves
Winchester
Hampshire
WR7 9PP

22nd March, 2006

Collège Public Jules Renard
16 r Christian d'Elva
53000 LAVAL
France.

(Dear Sir \ Dear Madam),

My family will be moving to this area (soon \ on 25\05\2006) and I am considering your school for my (child, Mary aged 12 \children Victor and Jane ages 13 and 15 respectively).

I have doctor's certificates for the children showing (their \ his \ her) vaccination dates for Tuberculosis and Diphtheria-Tetanus-Polio.

Perhaps you would be kind enough to contact (me \ us) to arrange for (me\us) to visit the school when we could discuss (his \ her \ their) academic and language skills.

Yours faithfully,

Gérard and Marion Broughton

There are many variables in this letter and care is needed to ensure accuracy. All options are in the same order in English and French.

25 The Groves
Winchester
Hampshire
WR7 9PP

Winchester, le 22 mars 2006

Collège Public Jules Renard
16 rue Christian d'Elva
53000 LAVAL
France

( Monsieur le Directeur \ Madame la Directrice ),

Ma famille emménage (bientôt \ le 25\05\2006) dans votre région et nous avons choisi votre établissement scolaire pour (notre enfant Mary âgée de 12 ans \ de nos enfants Victor et Jane ) âgés respectivement de 13 et 15 ans.

Le médecin m'a remis les certificats de (leurs \ ses) vaccins  tuberculose et diphtérie-tétanos-polio.

Nous vous serions reconnaissants de bien vouloir nous accorder un rendez-vous afin de visiter votre établissement et de discuter avec vous du niveau scolaire (de l'enfant \ des enfants ) ainsi que de (son \ sa \ leur) aptitude linguistique.

Dans l'attente de faire votre connaissance, veuillez agréer, (Monsieur le Directeur, \ Madame la Directrice,) l'expression de nos sentiments les meilleurs.

Gérard et Marion Broughton

# Changes to House Insurance Policy

There are many changes that may need to be made but these are two of the most common.

---

Les Petits-Bois
53872 - LAVAL

$12^{th}$ April, 2006

M. Jean Picard
Axa Assurances S.A.
Rue de Verdun
53540 Laval

Dear Sirs

### Policy No: AF1785642-107

I am writing to advise you that the property covered by the above policy will be rented from 01\06\05 for a period of 2 (months \ years).

Please advise me if there is any change in the premium rate.

I am writing to advise you that the property covered by the above policy will be used for business purposes relating to (type of business activity) from 01\06\05 for a period of 2 (months \ years).

Please advise me if there is any change in the premium rate.

Yours faithfully

Gerald and Marion Clements

*Rent House*

*Business Use*

Select the use required or edit to your own situation. Be careful to insert the correct dates, periods and business activity where appropriate.

Les Petits-Bois<br>
53872 - LAVAL

Laval, le 12 avril 2006

M. PICARD Jean
Axa Assurances S.A.
Rue de Verdun
53540 Laval

Monsieur,

**Police No: AF1785642-107**

Je viens vous faire savoir que la propriété couverte par la Police ci-dessus référencée sera louée à partir du 01\06\05 pour une période de 2(mois \ ans).

Je vous prie de m'informer de l'impact que ce changement va avoir sur le montant de la prime d'assurance et je vous en remercie bien vivement à l'avance.

Rent House

Je viens vous faire savoir que la propriété couverte par la police ci-dessus référencée va être utilisée à *(type of business activity)* à partir du 01\06\05 pour une période de 2 ( mois \ ans ).

Veuillez me faire savoir quelle répercussion ce changement va avoir sur la prime d'assurance.

Business Use

Avec mes remerciements anticipés, veuillez agréer,Monsieur, l'expression de mes meilleurs sentiments.

Gerald et Marion Clements

## Insurance repair quote

Accidents happen and you may need to obtain repair estimates.

---

Le Petit Bois
53567 Laval

2nd May 2006

Centre de Réparation d'Accidents
Rue de Laval
56350 MAYENNE

Dear Sirs,

### Vehicle Registration No: AS53 ABC

The above vehicle has been involved in an accident and I require a quotation for repair.

The cost or the repair is to be paid by (my insurance company \ myself).

Please advise of a date the repair could be started and how long the work will take.

Yours faithfully,

John Peterson

---

Just select who will be paying and you should soon have a quotation.

Le Petit Bois
53567 Laval

Laval, le 2 mai 2006

Centre de Réparation d'Accidents
Rue de Laval
56350 MAYENNE

Monsieur ,

### *Véhicule Immatriculé AS53 ABC*

Mon véhicule cité en référence a été impliqué dans un accident et je vous demande de bien vouloir me faire un devis de cette réparation.

Le coût de la réparation vous sera réglé directement (par ma compagnie d'assurance \ par moi-même).

Veuillez avoir l'obligeance de me dire quand vous pouvez réparer ce véhicule et le temps estimé pour effectuer cette réparation.

Veuillez recevoir, Monsieur, avec mes remerciements, l'expression de mes meilleurs sentiments.

John Peterson

## Insurance Claims

Sadly accidents happen and you might need to claim on you insurance policy.

Le Petit Bois
53567 Laval

2nd May 2006

Axa Assurance
3224 Avenue Jean-Béraud
Montpellier

Dear Sirs

**Policy No:   A298-9768-05**

I regret to inform you that my (car \ furniture \ buildings) have been damaged after (an accident \ a storm \ a flood \ a fire).  Would you please advise me as to the correct procedure and provide me with the appropriate claims forms.

I enclose the completed claim for the incident that occurred 03\03\2006, which I informed you of in my letter of 05\03\2006.

Enclosed are photographs that illustrate the damage.

Would you please process the claim as quickly as possible.

Yours faithfully,

Phillip Royal

Select the type of claim you are making and insert the appropriate date.

Le Petit Bois
53567 Laval

Laval, le 2 mai 2006

Axa Assurance
3224 Avenue Jean-Béraud
Montpellier

Monsieur,

### No Police:A298-9768-05

J'ai le regret de vous informer que (mon voiture \ mon meubles \ mon bâtiments) a été endommagé suite à ( un accident \ une tempête \ une inondation \ un incendie ) et je voudrais vous en faire la déclaration de sinistre.

Veuillez, s'il vous plaît, m'indiquer quelles sont les démarches que je dois entreprendre et m'adresser le formulaire de sinistre approprié.

Dans l'attente de votre réponse, je vous prie d'agréer, Monsieur, l'assurance de ma considération distinguée.

Je vous adresse sous ce pli la déclaration du sinistre survenu le 03\03\2006 dont je vous ai donné connaissance par lettre du 05\03\2006.

Je joins également les photos illustrant l'ampleur des dégâts.

Veuillez avoir l'obligeance de procéder au dédommagement le plus tôt possible.

Recevez, Monsieur, mes remerciements anticipés ainsi que mes sentiments les meilleurs.

Phillip Royal

Inform & get Claim Form

Send in Claim Form

## Insure House and Contents or Contents Only

Whilst you bank will almost certainly try to sell you insurance cover you will probably get a better deal on the open market.

25 The Groves
Winchester
Hampshire
WR7 9PP
United Kingdom

22nd  March, 2006

Axa Assurance
3224 Avenue Jean-Béraud
Montpellier

Cher Monsieur,

### **<u>Grand Mers, St Lucent, 66543 Montpellier</u>**

(I \ We) require building and contents insurance for the above property with a rebuild value of €200,000.

Your assistance in providing a quotation for a policy to cover  fire, storm, aircraft damage, civil liability etc. An application form would be greatly appreciated.

Should it be necessary for you to visit the property to check details of the house or contents please make an appointment . Our next visit to France will be 25\06\2006 to 28\06\2006

(I \ We) require household contents insurance for the above property with a maximum value of €60,000.  All risks cover of  €15,000 is required for  tv, videos, computers etc. including items used away from the property.

Your assistance in providing a quotation and application form would be greatly appreciated.

Yours faithfully,

Joan and Phillip Royal

Select the paragraph that you require and delete the unwanted (singular \
plural)
Make sure the amounts have been changed to suit you requirements.

25 The Groves
Winchester
Hampshire
WR7 9PP
United Kingdom

Axa Assurance
3224 Avenue Jean-Béraud
Montpellier

Winchester, le 22 mars 2006

Monsieur,

## Grand Mers, St Lucent, 66543 Montpellier

(Je désire \ Nous désirons) assurer (ma \ notre ) propriété citée en référence avec
une valeur de reconstruction de 2000000 € à neuf en cas de sinistre.( Bâtiment et
mobilier )

Voudriez-vous avoir l'amabilité de (m'adresser \ nous adresser) un spécimen de
police d'assurance comportant toutes les garanties nécessaires incendie, tempête,
vol, responsabilité civile etc..) et le montant de la prime annuelle.

S'il est nécessaire que vous visitiez cette propriété pour en vérifier surfaces et
nombres de pièces veuillez (me \ nous) le faire savoir et nous prendrons rendez-
vous sur place lors de (mon \ notre) prochain séjour en France.

(Je voudrais être assuré \ nous voudrions être assurés) contre le vol du mobilier et
objets de valeur contenus dans (ma \ notre ) propriété citée en référence avec un
maximum de valeur de 60000€. Nous voudrions nous assurer également pour les
appareils électriques suivants : tv, vidéos,ordinateur etc...d'une valeur de : 15000€
et tous les risques s'y referant également pour leur usage en dehors de la propriété.

Veuillez avoir l'amabilité de (m'adresser \ nous adresser) un spécimen de police
adéquate et (me \ nous ) faire connaître le montant de la prime annuelle en
découlant.

(Je vous en remercie \ Nous vous en remercions ) bien vivement à l'avance et vous
(prie \ prions) d'agréer, Monsieur, l'expression de (mes \ nos ) meilleurs
sentiments.

Phillip et Joan Royal

Building and Contents

Contents

# Health Insurance Top up Policy

With the French health system paying 70% of medical expenses this insurance can be vital.

Les Petits-Bois
53872 - LAVAL

12<sup>th</sup> April, 2006

ASSURANCES MARCEL PRATT INC.
1600 boul. St-Martin est
Bureau 800
Laval

Dear Sirs,

(I \ We) require top up mutuelles complémentaires medical insurance. Would you please be kind enough to provide a quotation for (me \ us) based on the following details

| | | | |
|---|---|---|---|
| Mrs Eva Clements | Female | Born: | 11\01\1967 |
| Mr Andrew Clements | Male | Born: | 10\11\1963 |
| Miss Lisa Clements | Female | Born: | 19\04\2000 |
| Mrs Andrew Clements | Male | Born: | 29\07\1991 |

Any information leaflets you have on this type of policy would be appreciated.

Yours faithfully

William Clements

Select the (singular \ plural) options and make sure to insert the date of birth of everybody to be included in the policy.

William Clements
Les Petits-Bois
53872 - LAVAL

Laval, le 12 avril 2006

ASSURANCES MARCEL PRATT INC.
1600 boul. St-Martin est
Bureau 800
Laval

Messieurs,

(Je souhaiterais \ Nous souhaiterions) souscrire à une assurance mutuelle complémentaire auprès de votre compagnie.
Voudriez-vous avoir l'amabilité d'établir une analyse financière pour (moi \ nous) compte tenu des informations suivantes:

| | | | |
|---|---|---|---|
| Madame Eva Clements | sexe féminin | née le | 11\01\1967 |
| Monsieur Andrew Clements | sexe masculin | né le | 10\11\1963 |
| Mademoiselle Lisa Clements | sexe féminin | née le | 19\04\2000 |
| Monsieur William Clements | sexe masculin | né le | 29\07\1991 |

Pourriez-vous avoir l'amabilité de bien vouloir (me \ nous) faire parvenir toute documentation sur ce genre de police d'assurance.

Recevez (mes \ nos) remerciements anticipés.

Veuillez agréer, Messieurs, l'expression de (mes \ nos) sentiments distingués.

William Clements

# Motor insurance quotation

Motor insurers in France may ask for proof of no accidents or claims for as long as ten years.

Le Petit Bois
Laval 53567

2nd May, 2006

Hérivaux Assureur
86, rue Victor Boissel
B.P.0816
53008 LAVAL Cedex


Dear Sirs,

### Volvo V40 2004  MU54YNT

I require motor insurance for the above vehicle with the following specification:

| | |
|---|---|
| Owner: | Name |
| age | sex |
| marital status | occupation |
| No claims bonus: | 12 years |
| Cover required: | (Comprehensive) (Third party fire and theft) |
| Convictions: | (none \ List convictions and dates, points) |
| Type of Licence: | (Full \ Provisional)   3 Points on Licence |
| Number of years Driving: | 17 |

| | |
|---|---|
| Other driver | Name |
| Age | Sex |
| Marital status | Occupation |
| Type of Licence: | (Full \ Provisional)  0 Points on Licence |
| Number of years Driving: | 8 |
| Accident record: | (None \ Date, claim value) |

Please let me have your quotation.


Yours faithfully,


John Matthews

Please take great care with any insurance details – inaccurate information, even accidentally may invalidate a policy.

Le Petit Bois
Laval 53567

Laval, le 2 mai 2006

Hérivaux Assureur
86, rue Victor Boissel
B.P.0816
53008 LAVAL Cedex

Messieurs,

### Volvo V40 2004  MU54YNT

Je désire assurer le véhicule cité en référence dont voici les renseignements:

Propriétaire:
Age:                                    Sexe:
Situation familiale                     Profession:
Pas d'accident:                         10 ans
Couverture demandée                     (Etendue \Tiers collision, incendie,
                                        vol, bris de glace)
Condamnation                            (Aucune\ *List convictions etc*)
Permis de conduire                      (plein \ provisoire) 3 points
Nombre d'années de conduite             17

Autre conducteur                        Nom, âge etc
Permis de conduire                      (plein \ provisoire) 0 points
Nombre d'années de conduite             8
Accidents enregistrés                   (Aucun \ *Date, claim value*)
Autre conducteur:

Veuillez me faire une proposition de prix.

Avec mes remerciements anticipés, veuillez agréer, Messieurs, l'expression de mes sentiments distingués.

John Matthews

# Book a Gite or Chambre d'hote (B & B)

It is normal practice to pay 10% deposit on booking and the balance either on confirmation of accommodation or arrival.

25 The Groves
Winchester
Hampshire
WR7 9PP

2<sup>nd</sup> September 2006

Dear Sirs,

(I \ We) would like to make a booking for your gite ref: 53290 at Domfront, France.

Please confirm that the gite has 3 bedrooms and beds for 5 people

Thank you for your assistance and (I \ we) look forward to your confirmation of availability and costs.

(I \ We) enclose payment of a 10% deposit and will pay the balance on receipt of your acceptance and invoice for the balance.

Your confirmation of this booking and directions of how to find the property would be appreciated.

Yours faithfully,

Yours faithfully,

Gerald and Marion Clements

There are a great number of (singular \ plural) choices – make sure you find them all!

25 The Groves
Winchester
Hampshire
WR7 9PP

Winchester, le 2 septembre 2006

Monsieur,

(Je voudrais \ Nous voudrions) faire une réservation dans votre ref: 53290 à Domfront, France.

Voudriez-vous avoir l'amabilité de (me \ nous) confirmer que votre dispose de: 3 chambres et des lits pour 5 personnes.

(Je vous remercie \ Nous vous remercions) de votre prochaine réponse (me \ nous) confirmant la réservation et le prix.

Veuillez (me \ nous) faire connaître le montant de l'acompte de 10% à vous verser en euros que (je vous réglerai \ nous vous réglerons) sitôt reçue votre confirmation.

Pourriez-vous également (m'adresser \ nous adresser) un plan ou (m' \ nous) indiquer l'itinéraire pour trouver facilement votre propriété?

(Je vous en remercie \ Nous vous en remercions vivement à l'avance et ( je serai \ nous serons ) très heureux de faire votre connaissance.

Recevez l'assurance de (mes \ nos) meilleurs sentiments.

Gerald et Marion Clements

## Enquiry for list of Gites – Hotels B & B

Address this to the tourist office of the town you wish to visit.

25 The Groves
Winchester
Hampshire
WR7 9PP

2nd September 2006

The Tourist Office
12, Place de la Roirie,
61700 DOMFRONT

Dear Sirs,

(I \ We) will be visiting France from 22\11\2006 to 30\11\2006 and are looking for (gite \ hotel \ Bed and Breakfast) accommodation.   Would you please let (me \ us) have a list of suitable accommodation.

The following are our requirements:

| | |
|---|---|
| Area | Normandy |
| Location | (Town \ rural \ coastal resort) |
| Number of people | 5 |
| Number of room required | 3 |
| Catering required | (Self catering \ half board \ full board) |

Thank you for your assistance and (I \ we) look forward to your reply.

Yours faithfully,

Gerald Clements

A lot of choices, adapt the accommodation requirements to your own and the usual (singular \ plural choices).

25 The Groves
Winchester
Hampshire
WR7 9PP

Winchester, le 2 septembre 2006

OFFICE DE TOURISME,
Place de la Roirie,
61700 DOMFRONT

Monsieur,

(Je voudrais \ Nous voudrions) visiter la France du 22\11\2006 au 30\11\2006 et (je recherche \ nous recherchons ) des (gîtes \ hôtels \ chambres d'hôtes) avec ou sans table d'hôtes. Voudriez-vous avoir l'amabilité de (m'en \ nous en) adresser une liste?

Les critères de (ma \ notre) recherche sont les suivants:

| | |
|---|---|
| Région ou Département | Normandie |
| Localité | (Ville \ Campagne \ Région côtière) |
| Nombre de personnes | 5 |
| Nombre de chambres recherchées | 3 |
| Genre de Service recherché | (Self service \ demi-pension \ pension Complète) |

(Je vous remercie \ Nous vous remercions) vivement à l'avance de votre réponse ainsi que de votre aide.

Veuillez agréer, Monsieur, l'expression de (mes \ nos) sentiments distingués.

Gerald Clements

# Make a Hotel or Chambre d'Hote Reservation

Family or group Booking

Single Person Booking

25 The Groves
Winchester
Hampshire
WR7 9PP

2$^{nd}$ April, 2006

Hotel De Bretagne
145 Rue Aristide-briand,
Pre En Pail, 53140 France

Dear Sirs,

We will be visiting France and would like to make a booking with you for the nights of 25\06\2006 to 28\06\2006 inclusive

The following are our requirements:

| | |
|---|---|
| Number of people | 5 |
| Number of room required | 3 |
| Catering required | breakfast \ half board \ full board. |

Thank you for your assistance and we look forward to your confirmation of availability and costs.

I will be visiting France and would like to make a booking with you for the nights of 25\06\2006 to 28\06\2006 inclusive.

Please reserve a single bedroom with (breakfast \ half board \ full board).

Thank you for your assistance and I look forward to receiving your confirmation of this booking.

Yours faithfully,

Peter Jamison

Select the correct paragraph for either group or single booking and change the dates to your needs.

25 The Groves
Winchester
Hampshire
WR7 9PP
Winchester, le 2 septembre 2006

Hotel De Bretagne
145 Rue Aristide-briand,
Pre En Pail, 53140 France

Messieurs,

Nous désirons visiter la France et voudrions prendre une réservation dans votre établissement  pour les nuits du 25\06\2006 au 28\06\2006 inclus.

Nous désirons:

| | |
|---|---|
| Nombre de personnes: | 5 |
| Nombre de chambres | 3 |
| Service recherché | nuitée avec petit-déjeûner \ demi-pension \ pension complète |

Nous vous remercions de vouloir bien prendre en note cette réservation, de nous en adresser confirmation et nous faire connaître le prix total de ce séjour.

Avec nos meilleurs sentiments.


J'ai l'intention de visiter la France et je souhaiterais prendre  une réservation dans votre Etablissement  pour les nuits du 25\06\2006 au 28\06\2006 inclus.

Je désire une chambre d'une personne pour nuitée (avec petit-déjeuner \ en demi-pension \ en pension complète)

Je vous remercie de vouloir bien prendre ma réservation en note et de m'en donner confirmation ainsi que le coût total de ce séjour.

Recevez, Monsieur, l'expression, de mes meilleurs sentiments.


Peter Jamison

Family or group Booking

Single Person Booking

## Arrange to Rent a House

The rental market in France is considerably stronger than the UK and most immobiliers and notaires have properties to let at rents far below UK rates.

25 The Groves
Winchester
Hampshire
WR7 9PP

22nd March, 2006

Premont Immobilier
4 rue du Parc
75000 - PARIS

Dear Sirs,

(I \ We) are looking to rent a property in the Montpellier area for a period of 6 months from 01\07\2006 whilst (I \ we) (look for a property \ renovate our house)

The property must have: 3 bedrooms 2 living rooms, garden, garage, car space 0.5 acres land area.

Please advise as to all suitable properties you have available and what references you will require.

Yours faithfully

Gérard and Marion Broughton

Apart from the singular \ plural choices and dates, be careful with the first paragraph - French grammar is more wordy than English. The room options and land etc should be changed to your own requirements.

25 The Groves
Winchester
Hampshire
WR7 9PP

Winchester, le 22 mars 2006

Premont Immobilier
4 rue du Parc
75000 - PARIS

Messieurs,

(J'ai \ Nous avons) l'intention de louer une propriété dans la région de Montpellier pour une période de 6 mois à compter du 01\07\2006; (je voudrais \ nous voudrions ) une propriété tandis que (je recherche \ nous recherchons) une propriété \ (je rénove \ nous rénovons) notre maison).

Cette location devra inclure 3 chambres, 3 salles de séjour, jardin, garage, parking et 0,5 ares de terrain autour.

Veuillez avoir l'amabilité de me prévenir dès que vous aurez une location de ce genre et me dire quelles références et garanties vous exigez.          \

Recevez (mes \ nos) remerciements anticipés pour la bonne suite que vous voudrez bien apporter à (ma \ notre) demande.

Veuillez agréer, Messieurs, l'expression de (mes \ nos) sentiments les meilleurs.

Gérard et Marion Broughton

## Cat and Dogs at the Vets

Forgetting vaccinations will lead to problems if you want to travel to or from the United Kingdom with pets.

---

Le Petit Bois
Laval 53567

22nd November, 2006

Cabinet Vétérinaire de Paris Nord
Rue de Santine
31005 PARIS

Dear Sirs,

**Vaccinations**

(My \ Our) (dog \ cat) requires vaccination for rabies to comply with the United Kingdom pet passport scheme and (I \ we) would ask that a suitable vaccination be given and a certificate issued to comply with the scheme.

**Ticks & Fleas**

(My \ Our) (dog \ cat) requires treatment for (ticks \fleas \ worms). Would you please supply and administer the required medication. Your advice as to when repeat treatment will be required would be appreciated.

Yours faithfully

John Matthews

---

Select the appropriate paragraph for vaccinations or ticks fleas and worms and make life more pleasant for your pets.

Le Petit Bois
Laval 53567

Laval, le 22 novembre 2006

Cabinet Vétérinaire de Paris Nord
Rue de Santine
31005 PARIS

Monsieur,

(Mon \ Notre) (chien \ chat ) doit être vacciné contre la rage pour observer les conditions de passeport avec animal de compagnie vers la Grande Bretagne.

Puis-je vous demander de bien vouloir effectuer cette vaccination et de me remettre un certificat conforme aux conditions U.K.

Vaccinations

(Mon\ Notre) (chien \ chat) doit subir un traitement contre les (tics \ puces \ vers).

Puis-je vous demander de prévoir ce médicament et de l'administrer à mon (chien \ chat).Veuillez me faire savoir également quand il nous faudra renouveler ce traitement si nécessaire.

Ticks & Fleas

Recevez, Monsieur, l'expression de (mes \ nos) sentiments les meilleurs.

John Matthews

## Union Nationale Accueils des Villes Françaises

The aim of the Association is to welcome individuals and families who have recently moved to a town or to the surrounding area and to ease their adaptation to their new way of life. There are 400 branches throughout France.

Les Petits-Bois
83872 – NANTES

22nd March, 2006

UNAVF
3 Rue du Paradis
75010 PARIS

Dear Sirs,

(I have \ We have) recently moved into Nantes and would be interested in making contact with your organisation. Could (I \ we) have the contact details of your group nearest to my new home.

(I \ We) understand the need to integrate with the local people and community and would appreciate your assistance at the beginning of (my \ our) life in France.

Yours faithfully,

Peter  Clements

Intergration into the local French community is essential and UNAVF provide help and guidance to enable an enjoyable introduction to life in France.

Les Petits-Bois
83872- Nantes

Nantes, le 22 mars 2006

UNAVF
3 rue du Paradis
75010 Paris

Messieurs,

(Je viens \ Nous venons) d'emménager à Nantes et (je souhaiterais\ nous souhaiterions) prendre contact avec votre organisme.
Pourriez-vous avoir l'amabilité de (me\ nous) faire parvenir les coordonnées du groupe le plus proche de notre nouveau domicile.

( Je suis consciente \ Nous sommes conscientes ) qu'il est essentiel de bien (m' \ nous) intégrer dans notre voisinage et notre communauté. C'est pourquoi (je vous serais infiniment reconnaissante \ nous vous serions infiniment reconnaissantes) de bien vouloir (m' \ nous) assister au commencement de (ma \ notre) vie en France.

Veuillez agréer, Messieurs, l'expression de (mes \ nos) sentiments distingués.

Peter Clements

## Accept or decline an invitation

Social occasions are an essential part of integrating in to the community and courtesy requires an answer to invitations.

Les Petits-Bois
53872 - LAVAL

12<sup>th</sup> April, 2006

Dear Friend(s),

**Accept**

Thank you so much for your kind invitation your (barbeque \ birthday party \ housewarming \ reception) at Laval on Saturday, May 21st.

We would be delighted to be there and look forward to meeting you again.

**Unable to accept**

Thank you so much for your kind invitation to the (barbeque \ birthday party \ housewarming \ reception) at Laval on Saturday, May 21st.

We wanted to be there to be with you for this but unfortunately we have (to be elsewhere \ already made other commitments that we cannot change).

Please be assured of our best wishes for this day and (I \ we) will be thinking of you.

Yours sincerely,

Gerald and Marion Clements

Select the acceptance or decline paragraphs and be careful about deleting the (singular \ plural) options.

Les Petits-Bois
53872 - LAVAL

Laval, le 12 avril 2006

Cher Ami \ Chers Amis),

(Je vous remercie \ Nous vous remercions) beaucoup de votre aimable invitation à participer à votre (barbecue\ anniversaire\ pendaison de crémaillère\ réception) à Laval le samedi 21 mai prochain.

(Je suis \ Nous sommes très heureux d'accepter votre invitation et de vous revoir.

(Je vous adresse \ Nous vous adressons) toutes (mes \ nos) amitiés.

Accept

(Je vous remercie \ Nous vous remercions) beaucoup pour votre aimable invitation à participer à votre (barbecue \ anniversaire \ pendaison de crémaillère \ réception ) à Laval  le samedi 21 mai prochain.

Malheureusement,( je suis désolé \ nous sommes désolés) de ne pouvoir être parmi vous parce que (je suis \ nous sommes) dejà engagé(s) pour une autre invitation  dont la date ne peut être modifiée.

(Je le regrette \ Nous le regrettons) vivement et (je vous adresse \ nous vous adressons) tous (mes \ nos) meilleurs voeux pour cette journée.

Recevez toutes (mes \ nos) amitiés.

Unable to accept

Gerald et Marion Clements

# Accept or decline a wedding \ christening invitation

French wedding and christenings celebrations are renown and to be invited is a wonderful way to integrate with the local community.

Les Petit Bois
53578 - Laval

15<sup>th</sup> May 2006

Dear Stéphane and Marie

Thank you so much for your kind invitation to the (dedication \ christening \ wedding) of your (daughter \ son \ grandson \ granddaughter) at Eglise Protestante Baptiste, Laval on Sunday, June 16<sup>th</sup>.

We would be delighted to be there and look forward to meeting you for this important ceremony.

Thank you so much for your kind invitation to the (dedication \ christening \ wedding) of your (daughter \ son \ grandson \ granddaughter) at Eglise Potestante Baptiste, Laval on Sunday, June 16<sup>th</sup>.

We wanted to be there to be with you for this important ceremony but unfortunately we have already made other commitments that we cannot change.

Please be assured of our best wishes for this occasion and (I \ we) will be thinking of you.

Yours sincerely,

Gerald and Marion Clements.

Check carefully to delete the unrequired events and relationships, both letters list the choices in the same order.

Remember the (singular \ plural) choices

Gérald et Marion Clements
Les Petits Bois
53578 - LAVAL

Laval, le 15 mai 2006

Chers Stéphane and Marie,

( Je vous remercie \ Nous vous remercions) vivement de votre aimable invitation (à  la consécration  \  au baptême \ au mariage ) de votre ( fille \ fils \ petit-fils \ petite fille ) en l'Eglise Protestante Baptiste de Laval le 16 juin prochain.

( Je suis \ Nous sommes) très heureux de vous confirmer que (j'assisterai \ nous assisterons) avec vous à cette importante cérémonie.

(Je vous adresse \ Nous vous adressons) toutes (mes \ nos) amitiés.

Accept Invitation

( Je vous remercie \ Nous vous remercions) vivement de votre aimable invitation (à  la consécration  \  au baptême \ au mariage ) de votre ( fille \ fils \ petit-fils \ petite fille )  en l'Eglise Protestante Baptiste de Laval le 16 juin prochain.

(Je suis navree \ Nous sommes navrées) de ne pouvoir assister avec vous à cette importante cérémonie car (je me suis déjà engagée \ nous nous sommes déjà engagées) pour une autre invitation dont la date ne peut être reportée.
(Je le regrette \ Nous le regrettons) vivement et (vous adresse \ vous adressons) tous (mes \ nos) meilleurs voeux pour la réussite de ce grand événement.

Recevez toutes (mes \ nos) amitiés.

Decline Invitation

Gérald et Marion Clements

# Announce a Wedding

Telling friends, French and English about a forthcoming wedding is important .

Gerald and Petra Jones
Les Petit Bois
10000 Laval

Laval, le 15 May 2006

Marion and Frederick Miles
Les Sables,
72341  Viron

Dear (Friend \ Friends \ Marion \ Marion and Frederick)

(I am \ We are) pleased to announce the marriage of our (daughter Françoise \ son Etienne) on September 15$^{th}$ in Laval.

You will shortly receive a formal invitation for the ceremonies and buffet, but I wanted to let you know as soon as possible to enable you to make a note in your diary.

 The civil marriage will take place at the town hall, Laval at 11.30 am and the church ceremony at  Eglise Potestante Baptiste, 13 Grande Rue, 53000  Laval at 2 pm.

(I \ We) hope you will be able to join us in celebrating this marriage.

Yours truly,

Gerald and Petra Jones

Remember to remove the unwanted alternatives and delete the brackets.
You would never believe the number of different ways to say "Dear ....."

| | | |
|---|---|---|
| Cher Ami | Dear male friend | **Gerald and Petra JONES** |
| **Chère** Amie | Dear female friend | **Les Petit Bois** |
| Chers Amis | Dear friends | 10000 - LAVAL |
| Cher Fred | Dear Fred | |
| **Chère Marion** | **Dear Marion** | |
| **Chers** Fred et Marion | Dear Fred and Marion | |

Laval, le 22 août 2004

Cher Ami \ Chère Amie \ Chers Amis \ Cher Jean \ Chers Jean et Marie-Cécile)

(Je suis \ Nous sommes) très heureux de vous annoncer le mariage de notre (fille Françoise \ fils Etienne) le 15 septembre prochain à Laval.

Vous recevrez bientôt un faire-part d'invitation aux cérémonies et buffet mais (je voulais \ nous voulions) vous en prévenir au plus tôt afin que vous puissiez prendre vos dispositions.

Le mariage civil aura lieu à la Mairie de Laval à 11.h.30 et la cérémonie religieuse en l'Eglise Protestante Baptiste, 13 Grande Rue - 53000 - Laval - à 14 heures.

(J'espère \ Nous espérons) que vous pourrez vous joindre à cette célebration de mariage.

Recevez toutes (mes \ nos) amitiés.

Gerald et Petra Jones

## Announce Birth of a Baby

Les Petits Bois
53501 - LAVAL

22nd August, 2006

Dear  Friends

(I am\ We are) delighted to tell you of  the birth of our (daughter \ son \ twins on August 10th at The Town Hospital in Laval.

*(I am \ We are) delighted to tell you of  the birth of our (granddaughter \ grandson \ twin grandchildren)  on August 10th at The Town Hospital in Laval.*

The (baby \ babies) weighed 3.2 kg and mother and (baby \ babies)  are both making wonderful progress.

The photo will be ready in a few days.

(I \ We) hope you will be able to visit us soon to meet the new arrival (s).

Yours sincerely,

Gérard and Marion Clements

Gérard et Marion CLEMENTS
Les Petits Bois
53501 - LAVAL

| **Careful With French Genders!** | |
|---|---|
| Cher Ami | (male friend) |
| Chère Amie | (female friend) |
| Chers Amis | (multiple friends) |
| Cher Peter | (Male name) |
| Chère Julia | (Female name) |
| Chers Jean at Marie | (Joint Names) |

Laval, le 22 août 2006

Cher (e) s Ami (e)s - ( Cher Jean - Chers Jean et Marie-Cécile ).

(Je suis \ Nous sommes ) très heureux de vous annoncer la naissance de notre ( fille \ fils \ nos jumeaux \ nos jumelles ) le 10 août dernier à l'hôpital de Laval.

*(Je suis \ Nous sommes ) très heureux de vous annoncer la naissance de notre ( petite fille \ petit fils \ de jumeaux \ de jumelles ) chez notre( fils Charles et Madeleine \ notre fille Caroline et Jacques ) le 10 août dernier à l'hôpital de Laval.*

(Le bébé pèse \ Les bébés pèsent )  3.2 kilos et maman et (bébé \ bébés ) sont en excellente santé.

La photo sera prête dans quelques jours.

(J'espère \ Nous espérons) que vous pourrez venir nous voir bientôt afin que nous fêtions cet heureux événement.

Toutes nos amitiés.

Gérard et Marion Clements.

# Offer Condolences

For those who would wish to include a spiritual message an alternative paragraph is shown in italics.

Les Petits Bois
53540 - LAVAL

15th May, 2006

Dear Pierre and Marie,

(I was \ We were) so sad to hear about the (sudden death \ tragic loss) of Jean Claude   (on 5<sup>th</sup> May \ yesterday \ last week).

This has shaken (me \ us) and (I \ we) feel deep sympathy for you in your loss.

Please be assured of our (thoughts \ prayers) at this time and if (I \ we) can be of any assistance just let us know.

*(I \ We) know that Jean Claude is now with (the Lord \ Jesus \ in heaven) and this must give you great assurance of future life.*

Yours sincerely,

Paul and Mandy James

On such a sensitive subject please take great care to select the correct (singular \ plural) choices and, if you use the spiritual paragraph remember to change the italics to match the other typeface.

Paul and Mandy James
Les Petits Bois
53540 - LAVAL

Laval, le 15 mai 2006

Chère Marie,
Cher Pierre,
Chers Pierre et Marie,

C'est avec beaucoup de peine que (j'ai \ nous avons) appris le (décès soudain \ la tragique disparition) de Jean-Paul (le 5 mai dernier \hier \la semaine dernière).

(J'en ai \ Nous en avons) été très profondèment attristé\e\s et (je vous adresse \ nous vous adressons) toute (ma \ notre ) sympathie en cette pénible circonstance.

Soyez assuré\e\s de (mes pensées \ nos prières) et si (je peux \ nous pouvons ) vous apporter aide et assistance n'hésitez pas à (m'appeler \ nous appeler ).      | 1 |

*(Je pense \ Nous pensons) que* Jean-Paul *est maintenant avec (le Seigneur \ Jésus \ au Paradis) cette pensée (m' \ nous ) aide à considérer l'avenir plus sereinement.*      | 2 |

Recevez toutes (mes \ nos) amitiés.

Paul et Mandy James

224

# Thanks for Condolences

For those who would wish to include a spiritual message an alternative paragraph is shown in italics.

---

Les Petits Bois
53540 - LAVAL

15th May, 2006

Dear Pierre and Marie,

Thank you so much for your kind words following the (sudden death \ tragic loss) of Jean-Claude  (on 5<sup>th</sup> May \ yesterday\ \last week).

Your kindness has been of great comfort to me and your friendship is greatly valued at this time.

**1** I thank you for your (thoughts \ prayers) at this time and (I \ we)hope to meet you again soon.

**2** *(I \ We) know that Jean-Claude is now with (the Lord \ Jesus \ in heaven) and with this knowledge (I \ we) will face the future with great assurance.*

Yours sincerely,

Paul and Mandy James

---

On such a sensitive subject please take great care to select the correct (singular \ plural) choices and, if you use the spiritual paragraph remember to change the italics to match the other typeface.

Paul et Mandy James
Les Petits Bois
53540 - LAVAL

Laval, le 15 mai 2006

Chère Marie,
Cher Pierre,
Chers Pierre et Marie,

Merci infiniment de votre aimable message faisant suite (au décès soudain de Jean Claude survenu \ à la perte tragique de Jean Claude survenue) (le 8 mai \ hier \ la semaine dernière ).

Votre sympathie a été d'un grand réconfort pour (moi \ nous) et votre amitié extrêmement appréciée en cet instant.

(Je vous remercie\ Nous vous remercions) de vos pensées (prières) en cette triste circonstance et (j'espère \ nous espérons) vous revoir très bientôt.

*(Je sais \ Nous savons) que Jean Claude est maintenant près de (Le seigneur \ Jésus \ au Paradis) et cette pensée (m '\ nous) aide à considérer l'avenir plus sereinement.*

Recevez toute (ma \ notre) reconnaissance.

Paul et Mandy James

1

2

## Father Christmas

Probably the most important letter in the book – especially if you are a child!

Les Petits-Bois
53872 - LAVAL

12<sup>th</sup> December, 2006

Father Christmas
Santas Workshops
The North Pole.

Dear Father Christmas,

How are you getting on with making presents for Christmas? Are Mrs Christmas and the elves helping you? Will you be coming to see me this year? So many questions.

I have tried to be good and well behaved and have tried to be gentle with my (brother \ sister \ pets). I have worked ever so hard at school and help my mummy with keeping my room tidy.

Last year you were very generous with so many presents and this year I am hoping that you might be able to bring me the latest Game Boy machine. If you can't I will be very happy with any present.

Please give Rudolph and his reindeer friends some extra hay for the long trip on Christmas eve and I have asked mummy and daddy to put a cake and a special drink for you near the chimney.

Lots of love and I really want to see you,

Peter Clements (aged three)

Please select the choice of who the writer has been nice to!

Les Petits-Bois
53872 - LAVAL

Laval, le 12 décembre 2006

Père Noël
Ateliers du Père Noël
Le Pôle nord

Cher Père Noël,

Où en êtes-vous avec votre fabrique de cadeaux pour Noël? Est-ce que Madame Noël et les elfes vous aident bien? Viendrez-vous me voir cette année? Tant de questions.

J'ai essayé d'être sage et de bien me comporter et aussi d'être très gentil avec ( mon frère \ ma soeur \ mes animaux). J'ai bien travaillé à l'école et j'ai aidé ma maman à ranger ma chambre avec soin.

L'année dernière vous avez été très généreux en cadeaux et cette année je pense que vous pourrez m'apporter la toute dernière console de jeux. Si vous ne le pouvez pas je me contenterais d'un autre cadeau.

N'oubliez pas, s'il vous plaît, de donner à Rudolphe et à ses amis rennes, le meilleur foin possible pour le long voyage de la veille de Noël et j'ai demandé à Maman et à Papa de laisser un gâteau et une bonne bouteille près de la cheminée.

Je vous fais plein de baisers et j'espère vous voir vraiment.

Peter Clements  (trois ans)

Printed in the United Kingdom
by Lightning Source UK Ltd.
120089UK00002B/147